Accession no

D1394350

Social interactions in urban public places

This publication can be provided in other formats, such as large print, Braille and audio. Please contact: Communications, Joseph Rowntree Foundation, The Homestead, 40 Water End, York YO30 6WP. Tel: 01904 615905. Email: info@jrf.org.uk

✔ Available in other formats

Social interactions in urban public places

Caroline Holland, Andrew Clark, Jeanne Katz and Sheila Peace

LIS LIBRARY

Date	Fund
01/06/17	g-Cue

Order No
2808006

University of Chester

JOSEPH ROWNTREE
FOUNDATION

First published in Great Britain in 2007 by

The Policy Press
Fourth Floor, Beacon House
Queen's Road
Bristol BS8 1QU
UK

Tel no   +44 (0)117 331 4054
Fax no   +44 (0)117 331 4093
Email   tpp-info@bristol.ac.uk
www.policypress.org.uk

© The Open University 2007

Transferred to Digital Print 2008

Published for the Joseph Rowntree Foundation by The Policy Press

ISBN 978 1 86134 997 2

British Library Cataloguing in Publication Data
A catalogue record for this book is available from the British Library.

Library of Congress Cataloging-in-Publication Data
A catalog record for this book has been requested.

Caroline Holland is a research associate, **Jeanne Katz** is Senior Lecturer and **Sheila Peace** is Professor of Social Gerontology – all in the Faculty of Health and Social Care, The Open University. **Andrew Clark** is a research fellow in the Leeds Social Sciences Institute, University of Leeds.

All rights reserved: no part of this publication may be reproduced, stored in a retrieval system, or transmitted in any form or by any means, electronic, mechanical, photocopying, recording or otherwise without the prior written permission of the Publishers.

The **Joseph Rowntree Foundation** has supported this project as part of its programme of research and innovative development projects, which it hopes will be of value to policy makers, practitioners and service users. The facts presented and views expressed in this report are, however, those of the authors and not necessarily those of the Foundation.

The statements and opinions contained within this publication are solely those of the authors and not of the University of Bristol or The Policy Press. The University of Bristol and The Policy Press disclaim responsibility for any injury to persons or property resulting from any material published in this publication.

The Policy Press works to counter discrimination on grounds of gender, race, disability, age and sexuality.

Cover photograph: Kippa Matthews
Cover design by Qube Design Associates, Bristol
Printed in Great Britain by Marston Book Services, Oxford

Contents

List of maps, photographs and tables

Maps

Photographs

Tables

Acknowledgements

The authors would like to thank the Joseph Rowntree Foundation for funding this study as part of the Public Spaces Programme, in particular Katharine Knox. The co-researchers (also known as observers) provided very rich data and were instrumental in making choices about the direction of the study, and we are very grateful for their dedication and interest. Aylesbury Vale District Council was constant in its support for the study and provided contacts as well as guidance throughout. Thanks are also due to the advisory group whose feedback at the different stages of the study was invaluable. The group included: Demelza Birch, Josephine Brader, Dr Elizabeth Burton, Suzanne Cheshire, Dan Clucas, Rachel Conner, Barbara Eccleston, Dr Peter Rogers, Chris Schmidt-Reid, Dr Katherine Southwell and Talia Sulman. We would like to thank the people who gave us permission to take photographs of them or to interview them. Finally, we are indebted to the people of Aylesbury who in going about their daily lives enabled this creative project to happen.

The photographs in this report were taken by Kippa Matthews (kippamatthews@yahoo.co.uk).

Summary

This research focuses on the use of different public (and pseudo-public) spaces in urban areas.[1] It draws on a case study of a year-long research project in the town of Aylesbury in southeast England, a market town with a population of around 69,000. The study set out to examine how different people use public spaces and to analyse how social interactions vary by age, gender or place. What it does not do, is reflect what is known about these different groups' use of other 'spaces', for example their own homes and other indoor facilities. The findings were considered in terms of their relevance for emerging policy agendas on shared and contested spaces, intergenerational relationships, safety and security, and the management of public space.

The project is based on a mixed-methods approach, which involved discussion with a wide range of stakeholders in the town, from local politicians and community leaders to business owners and managers; street surveys with members of the public at a range of observations sites; and non-participant observation at nine sites, undertaken by 46 members of the general public (aged 16-73 years) over a 12-month period (October 2004 to September 2005). The observations were carried out in three types of public spaces: residential neighbourhoods, green open spaces and town centre spaces, which were considered representative of the town's public spaces as a whole. The observations were carried out across the day from 7am to 1am. The research method was highly participatory, with the observers also contributing to and informing the data analysis.

Similarity and difference in the use of public space

Public spaces allow people to meet on ostensibly neutral ground in planned and unplanned ways, to interact with others within the context of the whole community. These include family relationships (for example, multi-generation family shopping expeditions), cultural groupings (for example, youth groups), local social connections (for example, chance or planned meetings with friends, neighbours and work colleagues) and groups meeting through common interest (for example, walking groups). By facilitating this mixing, public spaces can contribute to the cohesion of communities. There was little evidence of overt conflict in the public spaces examined in this work. However, observations suggest that difference between groups can lead to self-segregation in the use of particular spaces and that perceptions of difference and particular behaviours by different users can mean that spaces can be divisive as well as inclusive. The public visibility of different kinds of people is underpinned by their presence in public spaces, and people's understanding of their community is in part formed by who and what they see in the public domain. Observation shows that many people use public spaces as opportunities for sanctioned people-watching. Visitors and residents from different parts of the town, including people from different ethnic and socioeconomic groups and people of different ages and abilities, can be in the same place at the same time, allowing people to assess and reassess the characteristics of space and their own relationship with it.

---

[1] In this report, the term 'space' is used to refer to the public locations and sites researched. When referring to the social constructions or representations of such spaces, the term 'place' is used.

This particularly applies in the case of ethnicity and cultural diversity in a town where the black and minority ethnic population is relatively small. Observation here shows fewer inter-ethnic social interactions among adults than among youths. The public spaces in the town centre provide locations where different groups within and between different age groups co-exist and observe each other even if they have little direct interaction.

People who are regarded as on the margins of respectable society, including those who are homeless, and street or underage drinkers and users of illegal drugs, were observed to have an ambiguous relationship with the rest of society in public spaces. By various means, ranging from control orders to the attitudes of other users, they are discouraged from some sites but tolerated in others. Specific public spaces act as their daytime social spaces and meeting points. These preferred spaces are observed to offer some privacy or seclusion along with a degree of security and connectedness with the town. Some individuals on the other hand maintain a highly visible presence in town centre spaces because they are often seen in the same place at regular times. Whether or not their presence is welcomed, these individual 'characters' become part of the familiar street scene. The practice of moving marginalised people such as street drinkers on from some areas displaces rather than deals with problems.

Intergenerational issues

People like to remain connected with the public life of their villages, towns and cities. This particularly applies to older people, and those who do not have other connections through places of work or education. Socially inclusive public spaces enable people of all ages to access essential services and facilities without physical barriers, safety concerns or transport difficulties in reaching them.

Young people in their teenage years have a particular need to be able to gather together in public spaces where they can practise sociability on neutral ground. However, to many adults, including area managers, such gatherings can produce unease and represent a potential source of petty crime and disorder. Many adults regard large groups of young people as a threat. Observation in this study showed, however, that most of the time, groups of young people are self-managing and benign. Rather than prohibiting gatherings of young people in public spaces, greater understanding of cultural issues between the generations could reduce feelings of threatening behaviour.

Some groups of younger people tend to select and colonise particular public spaces or structures as meeting points. This process can be seen as part of their practice of youth identity and it contributes to the development of their sense of place as they move into adulthood. Observation showed that the spaces young people selected incorporated an element of seclusion or separation, although they also sought a sense of security from the threat of what might be perceived to be 'dangerous others'. The design of both town centre and local public spaces should incorporate and recognise their need for space that invites privacy but remains legitimate and safe.

There are similarities and differences in behaviour across the generations. While observation revealed that older people use public spaces at different times to younger people – being more likely to be seen earlier in the day – some are particularly sensitive to the presence of others in public places. As a result they tend to remove themselves from areas that are heavily used by older children and young adults. Older people, like others, may also tend to avoid places that are dark or deserted. Survey data suggest that older people are reassured by the presence of visible security personnel.

Observation in public places shows little overt interaction between people of different generations who are strangers, although families including different generations were often seen, particularly in town centre areas. However, inclusive public spaces allow people of different generations to co-exist in ways that may mitigate expectations of trouble between them.

Managing public spaces

There is a consensus between statutory authorities, town and shopping centre managers and the general public that security is a major consideration in public spaces. Most people are observed to adhere to security regulations most of the time, and without this self-regulation public spaces would become unmanageable. However, where regulations are perceived as relating more to the convenience of management than to safety as such, the rules are more likely to be broken. For example, people were observed cycling in the deserted park; gathering in groups in the shopping centre; and playing ball games in local neighbourhood centres. This research suggests a need for some gradation of regulation in public places, drawing on community support and harnessing the general inclination of people to self-regulate to avoid conflict.

People are drawn to, and tend to stay longer in, public spaces that offer interest and stimulation and/or a degree of comfort. Survey and observation data show that people appreciate and look for special events and activities in public spaces, both locally and in the town centre. Unique and special events, including spontaneous 'street entertainment', also grab the attention and help to define places as interesting. People are more likely to linger if there is somewhere comfortable to sit, especially if there is also some protection from the weather.

However, it is also true that some people look for less regulated space. In Aylesbury this included the canal side of the town, which allowed people to enjoy a sense of tranquillity and appreciation of nature, while benefiting from proximity to the town centre. Canal corridors provide rare and unusual urban public spaces and they need protection from unsympathetic development. Towns and cities with canals should be helped to preserve them and to develop them thoughtfully and in consultation with users and local residents.

From interviews, surveys and observation it is clear that spaces acquire reputations (that is, as 'places') that may or may not be deserved, but which are persistent and which have an effect on whether and how people use those spaces. A reputation for crime or disturbance, once acquired, may be difficult to dislodge without positive action. The reputation of a place can have a serious effect on its economic development as well as how people feel about it; it is therefore important for reputation to be taken seriously.

Designing public spaces

Even where they are physically accessible, other aspects of public spaces can present barriers to their use by some people. In addition to regulations, these include location, and the provision or lack of facilities. For example, in this case study town, the municipal park is difficult to get to from the high street for less mobile people, and it is not well signposted. The scarcity of (open) public toilets in the town centre also presented a problem for many older people and parents of very young children, and, in surveys, the removal of public toilet facilities was a contentious issue. The parking of cars in the central public space of a newly developed housing estate was a serious impediment to the use of that area by young children and families using the shops, nursery and community centre.

The siting and location of street furniture was observed to have a marked effect on how it was used. Benches positioned with good viewpoints and 'something to look at' were heavily used by all kinds of people. Those located less conveniently, for example in a windy or less attractive position, were often ignored in favour of improvised seating on walls. The design of seating (for example whether multiple- or single-seater) had an effect on who used it and design needs to accommodate people's physical requirements. For example, comment was made on the need for benches with backs and armrests that would support frailer bodies and be of value to all. Without these facilities (especially in the case of toilets) some people will not linger or not venture out at all.

Signs in public spaces are often prohibitive or regulatory. While these notices are sometimes required for legal or health and safety reasons, observation showed that prohibitions that appeared to be arbitrary or unreasonable were often ignored. Public signage can also be informative, and the absence of good way-finding signage meant that visitors to the town could be unaware of places of interest in the town centre area, and visitors to the housing estate would have difficulty in locating the local centre.

Maintaining inclusion; avoiding exclusion

Public spaces were used differently according to the degree to which they were predominantly simple (undifferentiated) or complex (with different and contrasting parts). In wide open spaces most people tended to skirt the edges of the space unless there was an activity in progress. In more complex spaces, individuals and groups were able to position themselves more specifically, which could lead to the exclusion of others. For example, the formal garden section of the park offered vantage points where different groups (young people, homeless/drinkers' groups) could be alongside each other and observe each other without necessarily interacting. Focal points and landmarks that helped to define and punctuate spaces, even when they were controversial, were observed to draw people in.

In order to educate people about the role and possibilities for public spaces and its importance to democracy, central and local government need to increase public awareness of the issues by giving a higher profile to how public space is transformed and the ways in which people can become involved in planning and creating public places.

Towns need to establish places where activities can take place and groups can go where they will feel secure and free – including places for young people, people who want to drink and homeless people. It is important to question whether it is better to have spaces with people who are 'doing nothing' than spaces that are 'doing nothing' because there is no one present.

The vibrancy of towns, just as much as cities, depends on stimulation and challenge. While regeneration can provide pristine public spaces, it is the people that make the places. This research suggests that effective regeneration requires a sophisticated understanding of and engagement with users and potential users, particularly those living locally, who will be most involved in place-making.

Background

This chapter outlines some ways of thinking about public space in research and policy arenas. In the UK, public space can be considered ostensibly neutral ground, which is open to all. In practice, it varies widely in the ways it is used by different groups and individuals; the concepts of 'public' and 'space' both being open to interpretation and contestation (Briggs, 1963; Sennett, 1974; Habermas, 1989; Goheen, 1998). Individual usage and social interactions in public spaces are influenced by many factors, including how the spaces connect and the design, maintenance and management of the natural and the built environment. These issues and related policy initiatives are considered in more depth below.

Understanding public space

Central and local governments and numerous voluntary organisations have expressed commitment to the idea of providing public spaces in the UK. Studies have shown that a good-quality public realm can benefit local economies, encourage people to spend more time in shops and businesses, and raise house prices. Public spaces are regarded as democratic because everybody can use them: places that, rhetorically at least, allow 'community' to exist and flourish. Public space is 'our open-air living room, our outdoor leisure centre' (Lipton, 2002, Foreword), important to the health and well-being of residents of all ages.

Claiming social space and being seen in public becomes a way for social groups to legitimate their right to belong in society. Yet because they can be used by everyone, public spaces are frequently considered contested spaces; places where opposition, confrontation, resistance and subversion can be played out over 'the right to space' (Mitchell, 1995, 2003). These contestations may involve people from a range of social groups based on gender, age, ethnicity, sexuality, (dis)ability, social class and so on (Valentine, 1996; Malone, 2002). They may centre on the different meanings attached to different spaces, or draw on deeper struggles about social representations, or collective 'myths', about spaces (Cresswell, 1996).

How spaces are understood and used may also depend on individual and group characteristics (see, for example, Mitchell, 1995; Laws, 1997; McDowell, 1999; Low, 2000; Matthews et al, 2000). For instance, the sociology of childhood (James et al, 1998; www. openspace.eca.ac.uk/projects.htm) identifies public spaces as places where children and young people can construct a form of privacy in their own places, away from the familial control and surveillance of home (Malone, 2002). Thus, public spaces are imbued with power relations: particular social groups can be encouraged, tolerated, regulated, and sometimes excluded from public space depending on the degree to which they might be deemed 'in' or 'out of place'. For instance, acts such as loitering, drinking, skateboarding or even 'hanging out' in public may be constructed as inappropriate because of particular social representations about what sorts of groups, and activities, should be seen out in public (Wilson, 1991; Valentine, 1996). Consequently, the right to 'be' not just 'in public', but also 'a part' of that public is an important way in which different groups can assert their own legitimacy to belong. To be part of the public sphere, it has been argued, is thus at the heart of any inclusive democracy.

Laws (1997), considering age as a defining domain, has argued that our identities are constructed as much as by material acts – what we do – as by discursive practices – what we say. Who uses which spaces and how can influence societal attitudes to what is appropriate and who has 'ownership' of particular places at given times. Places have their own identities and histories, which, if known to those occupying them, may have an effect on how they are used. On the other hand, people using public spaces that are unknown to them may experience a range of emotions from curiosity to uncertainty to insecurity, which can also affect behaviour. Consequently, the processes by which 'individuals' and 'groups' compete for access to, or domination of, public spaces are much more complex than simple issues of public order or design. The ways in which space is socially produced is therefore essential to an understanding of how individuals and groups engage with public space.

Policy and practice issues

England (and Wales) has been subject to a large array of pro urban living planning policies, White Papers and good practice guides (DETR, 1998, 1999, 2000, 2001; Urban Task Force, 1999). With the emergence of notions of sustainable development there has been a general trend towards making urban environments more attractive places in which to live, both for existing residents, and for future generations, and the Urban White Paper (DETR, 2000) suggests an integrated action response, involving better design and planning, dealing with contaminated and disused land, promoting new investment and enterprise, improving environmental protection, providing more urban leisure opportunities such as parks, play areas and public spaces, and increasing the safety and attractiveness of the streets. In each case, the aim is to promote an environment that facilitates 'good urban living' (Stead and Hoppenbrouwer, 2004). Of concern here is the future of public space in contributing to this process.

'The state of open space in our towns and cities remains a serious blight, diminishing the quality of life of their citizens' (Transport, Local Government and the Regions Committee, 2002[2]). This comment was made in national planning guidance on public space in 2002 prior to the government's allocation of £89 million from the Sustainable Communities Plan to tackle the state of parks and public spaces. It demonstrates a belief in the social and economic benefits of inclusive and well-ordered public places – a view that is reflected in the language of the subsequent reports *Living Places: Cleaner, Safer, Greener* (ODPM, 2002) and *Living Places: Powers, Rights, Responsibilities* (DEFRA, 2002), which begin to develop coherent policies concerning the design and management of public spaces.

The 'cleaner, safer, greener communities' agenda encourages local authorities to create quality public spaces, (informed by research) that people will want to use – encouraging a sense of ownership. Here particular attention is given to the role of parks and urban green spaces as areas that will enhance quality of life for the whole community, and to how the lives of towns and city centres can be developed to encompass the evening and night-time economy (www.cleanersafergreener.gov.uk). Implicit in this is an understanding that alongside 'green spaces' there should also be a concern for streets, market squares and the ad hoc urban spaces of city landscapes within housing schemes, and also those spaces such as shopping malls where private enterprise co-exists with public thoroughfares. In

---

[2]   www.parliament.the-stationery-office.co.uk/pa/cm200102/cmselect/cmtlgr/238/23803.htm

recognition of this, the Commission for Architecture and the Built Environment (CABE) has recently extended its interests to reflect more fully the need to consider a wide range of public spaces rather than just green spaces in terms of design issues.

While there has been extensive research into the links between antisocial behaviour and public spaces (Newman, 1972; Coleman, 1990), less has been said about the social nature of these spaces. Antisocial behaviour, however defined, is felt more acutely in urban areas, particularly more deprived urban areas (DETR, 1998; Audit Commission, 2006). Some public spaces, particularly in town centres, have also faced difficulties associated with alcohol and drug use, the homeless and other 'undesirable' individuals. Drawing on the recommendations of Newman (1972) and Coleman (1990) among others, attempts have been made to 'design out' these problems by making public spaces unwelcoming, removing seating, preventing eating and regulation to deter loitering. Yet by making public space unattractive to these groups, so it becomes unattractive to many other potential users, and the actual 'problems' are not resolved, merely removed at best. By contrast, policy agendas on social inclusion and social cohesion, such as the Social Exclusion Unit's programmes on Mental Health and Young Adults with Troubled Lives, have been aimed at removing barriers to the social inclusion of some groups often considered 'undesirable' users of public spaces, while the programme on Excluded Older People addresses one of the major 'invisible' groups (ODPM, 2005a). These initiatives suggest the need for a more fundamental approach to consider the public visibility and inclusion of marginalised groups and the regulation of behaviours in contested spaces. The process carried out in this study, of observing what people do where, contributes to understanding how social interactions occur and the connections in seemingly disparate elements of the urban environment.

The public realm is diverse and while issues of public (dis)order and criminality have been identified as leading to greater regulation and policing for particular members of the community, not enough attention has been paid to the causes of (dis)order; the *shared* or *contested* use of spaces and the extent to which they may foster or inhibit a sense of community. Games, the use of non-motor vehicles, music, the mere congregation of particular groups – or indeed individuals – and many other legitimate uses of public space by one set of people may influence the behaviour of others. Understanding the social interactions between people within urban public spaces may thus be the starting point from which to develop practices that may realise some of the rhetoric of policy. It also requires acceptance of the view that 'all strategies should be based on research, understanding the community needs and wants, what is financially achievable and genuine determination and follow through' (www.cleanersafergreener.gov.uk/en/1/thinkstrategically.html).

2

'Social interactions in urban public places': aims and methods

The study presented here set out to examine how different people use their local public spaces in an urban area, in order to inform the policy and practice agendas discussed in Chapter 1. The research focused on the rhythms of public life in the town of Aylesbury with the aim of finding out how different sorts of public spaces are understood, managed and used relative to others within a single town. The study covered a range of different types of spaces, including residential areas, green spaces and town centre areas, including high streets and shopping malls.

The findings provide research of value to the citizens of Aylesbury concerning the needs of their town, but they also have implications for other areas that are experiencing similar issues within their public places. For instance, there are two prominent narratives in current writing and thinking on public space in Europe and North America. One refers to the apparent decline of public space, linked to processes such as privatisation, regulation and surveillance. The other offers a less pessimistic view, of public spaces enabling diverse groups to come together to display their identities in the public arena. There thus appears a paradox between public spaces as sites where difference is being eliminated, and sites where difference can be celebrated (Sennett, 1974; Sorkin, 1992; Zukin, 1995; Mitchell, 2003).

This debate raises a number of questions that are of interest to the specific case study presented here. Is public space disappearing in Aylesbury? Have privatised shopping centres replaced the high streets as the central public areas in the town? Do the town squares command positions as the centre of the social life of the town? Have particular groups been removed from the public spaces of the town or is there an environment where difference can be encountered in safe, non-threatening ways? Have specific social groups appropriated different spaces of the town, perhaps at different times of day or night? And in turn, how might these processes themselves be supported and reproduced by public spaces? What are the rhythms of public life in the town? Who participates in these rhythms? When can they be observed? And who is missing from them, and consequently hidden from the public life of the town?

This study considers some of these questions and reflects previous research that notes:

> The meaning of public space ... will be understood only by paying attention to the often confusing or seemingly trivial contests over the use and enjoyment of public space, whether old streets or new parks and cemeteries. (Goheen, 1998, p 493)

Aims and objectives

The primary aims and objectives of this research were:

- to examine how different social groups interact in key public spaces within a closely defined urban area;
- to analyse whether interactions differ with age or with place; and whether the presence of particular people or groups affects the use of public space by other people or groups;
- to relate analysis of social interactions to the emerging policy agendas concerning shared and contested use of space; intergenerational interaction; safety and security in public areas; management and maintenance of public space; and developing community research;
- to influence local initiatives to develop the use of public space by diverse users.

Methods

A mixed-methods approach was adopted, which consisted primarily of non-participative observation by the authors and a large team of co-researchers recruited from the local area (also referred to as observers) in nine key sites in Aylesbury (see Chapter 4). In addition, the authors conducted stakeholder interviews and a series of street surveys. The sites selected for observation included town centre squares, suburban shopping centres, central shopping malls, high streets, playing fields, parks and residential areas.

Non-participant observation

A non-participative, semi-structured observation method was devised for recording basic data about the characteristics, location and activities of groups and individuals within the observation sites. The public spaces selected for observation were too large and complex to observe without further subdivision into 'micro-sites'. For each micro-site an observation sheet was devised that comprised an outline diagram of the key features of the site, and a matrix on which observers could record demographic characteristics of people using the site and any interactions between them.

Observations took place from October 2004 to September 2005, across all days of the week and in all weathers (see Appendix). In addition to the authors, 46 people aged from 16 to 73 years took part in the observations at some point, and a core group observed throughout most of the study. Observers (co-researchers) usually worked in pairs for reasons of safety and they were paid by the hour. One observer completed the observation sheet while the other completed an 'ethnographic diary' to capture a wider representation of activity at the site. The observers received initial training and ongoing support, and many of them took part in debriefing sessions at which they were invited to reflect on their work. Most of the observations were carried out between 8am and 9pm, although a few were conducted up to 1am in the town centre locations.

The observation strategy was driven by a desire to get a little closer to 'what really happens' in public spaces as an expansion on more commonly researched aspects of what people think happens, or what people say happens within them. It required observers to feel safe, and to be as unobtrusive as possible so as to produce a record of 'real life' in the town, although due of the length of the study, many observers inevitably became recognised around the town. What was observed is not claimed to be a complete or always entirely 'natural' representation of activities by groups and individuals.

Stakeholder interviews

A range of individuals who might be expected to have an informed opinion about social interactions in specific places in Aylesbury or about the town in general were interviewed using a question schedule. These stakeholders included:

- local government officials (town centre, local centres, and race relations): 8
- local councillors and elected representatives: 2
- local non-governmental organisations/community representatives: 2
- shopping centre managers: 2
- security personnel: 2
- other business owners/managers: 8
- street drinkers and homeless people: 4

The opinions they gave were confidential and personal, and they are recorded in this report without specific attribution.

Street surveys

Street surveys were conducted at some of the observation sites to ask the general public about their use of specific spaces and their opinions about them. These were intended to produce data indicative of attitudes rather than statistically powerful data on the total footfall within each place. A total of 179 interviews were conducted using semi-structured survey instruments. Respondents were selected to try to cover as wide a range of people as possible in terms of age, gender and ethnicity. Some respondents took the opportunity to talk about the places in more detail and some of these comments are included in this report. The survey instrument was piloted in Market Square during February 2005. Surveys were conducted in the following May (town centre areas and Fairford Leys) and August (at Walton Court, Fairford Leys, Vale Park and High Street).

Feedback from co-researchers

As part of the data-gathering and analysis process, co-researchers were involved in two ways:

- At two points during the observation period (February and June) all co-researchers were invited to group sessions to discuss their observations, their interpretations of what they had seen and their experiences in the field.
- Following the completion of the observations, co-researchers were contacted individually, primarily by telephone, and interviewed about their experience of taking part in the project, their reasons for becoming involved and the skills they had developed.

Making sense of the data

Despite the somewhat structured nature of the observations, it is important to recognise that much of the data collected was subjective and dependent on the perceptions and points of view of the individual observers. This was recognised by some observers, although on the whole they also acknowledged that a particular 'way of seeing' was called for, as the following quotes from feedback interviews with observers illustrate:

'There was more to it than I thought originally; you needed to be on the ball.'

'[I was] seeing something that is very familiar in quite a different way. I use these places everyday and when you have to look at it and see who uses it, you see it in a very different light.'

'It was interesting for me because it is very sensory and subjective, which makes it quite unlike the type of work that I am used to.'

Some aspects of the observation method appeared to be 'more subjective' – or 'problematic' – than others. For example, many observers were concerned that they could not accurately record ages, ethnicities or 'social class'. For example, 'older people' were defined by individuals through cumulative characteristics such as appearance and speed of mobility. The data constructed in the observations were not taken as an objective truth but rather as a particular individual's view of events. One observer was particularly interested in this issue:

'[I worked] with an older woman and an Asian girl and that was really interesting to see what she thought about life, and how her religion affected her life. It helped me to understand a bit about this girl's reality. It was good to see anthropology in action.'

It was not the aim of the research to assess the accuracy with which observers can identify particular social and demographic characteristics. Rather, the study was concerned with the ways in which particular groups, and their activities and interactions, were interpreted by different observers. Consequently, the language and labels adopted by the observers are maintained in the following chapters.

However, the depth and degree of subjectivity should not be taken to imply that no trends, patterns or themes emerged from the data. By considering each observation chart and diary in relation to others produced in the same site at different times of the day, week or year, it was possible to construct a composite of layered accounts of a 'year in the life' of each public space. This, combined with data collected through the questionnaire and interview methods, together with feedback from the observers, allowed for triangulation and the construction of fuller accounts. Although the data do not claim to be 'the whole truth' about public spaces in the town, several key narratives emerged from the year in the research field. Some of these narratives are presented in the chapters that follow.

3

Introducing the study location

This chapter explains the rationale for selecting the study location, and the particular public spaces observed. Of course, no town is exactly the same as another, but many share similarities. This study aimed to look in depth at one town, to explore issues that might relate to towns elsewhere, rather than sampling in less depth across a number of towns. Aylesbury, the county town of Buckinghamshire in southeast England, was selected as the location for the study for a number of reasons. Its town centre area is compact and comprises a range of types of public places within easy walking distance of each other, ranging from central market squares to canal towpaths, and with post-war and more recent housing estates within two or three miles of the town centre. Aylesbury is neither particularly deprived nor affluent; it is the kind of location that is often overlooked in popular, academic and political discourses. Insofar as any town can be called 'ordinary', it was this apparent 'ordinariness' that suggested it as the location for the study. Map 1 shows the location of Aylesbury within England.

Map 1: Location of Aylesbury in England

Characteristics of Aylesbury

The county of Buckinghamshire is divided into four districts, including Aylesbury Vale, the major town of which is Aylesbury. The Aylesbury Vale District as a whole had a very slightly younger demographic than the average for England in the 2001 Census. Children and young people aged under 19 years formed 26.5% of the population in Aylesbury Vale (25% in England); while people aged over 65 formed 13% (compared to 16% in England). Ninety-four per cent of the population was white, the majority of the remaining population being of Asian origin. Between 1982 and 2002 the population of Aylesbury Vale increased by 24%, more than double the 11% increase for the South East region.

In recent decades, the town has increasingly become a commuter settlement for London, offering good rail and road links to the capital, yet with the attractions of (relatively) cheaper housing, schools with good reputations and the lure of open countryside, including the Chiltern Hills. Population growth is beginning to place demands on existing infrastructure and the town is scheduled for further growth over the next two decades as part of the southeast expansion plan. The 2001 population estimate for Aylesbury town was 69,000, but the subregional strategy calls for an increase of 15,000 more dwellings by 2021 with a concomitant increase in the town's population. These new homes will add to the patchwork of socio-spatial segregation since the development of a number of social housing estates after the Second World War. The town's economic stability increasingly lies with the tertiary (service) and quaternary (knowledge-based) sectors.

Public spaces in Aylesbury and introduction to sites chosen for observation

The study drew on Madanipour's (1999) definition of public space, which includes those areas physically accessible to all, regardless of ownership, where people can enter with few restrictions. In order to include a representative range of different kinds of spaces, a typology of public spaces in Aylesbury was developed. This was informed by existing space typologies including those proposed by Kit Campbell Associates (2001). The Aylesbury sites were selected to cover as broad a range as possible within the typology (Table 1).

Table 1: Typology of public spaces in Aylesbury

	Canal towpath	Fairford Leys	Friars Square	Hale Leys	High Street	Kingsbury	Market Square	Walton Court	Vale Park
Indoor			X	X					
Outdoor – undeveloped	X								
Outdoor – developed		X			X	X	X	X	
Green space	X							X	X
Commercial and civic space			X	X	X	X	X		
Residential space		X						X	
Recreational space	X							X	X
Public space	X	X			X	X	X	X	X
Quasi-public space			X	X					
Neighbourhood centre		X						X	
Town centre	X		X	X	X	X	X		X

The juxtaposition of the town centre locations is shown in Map 2.

Map 2: Juxtaposition of town centre locations

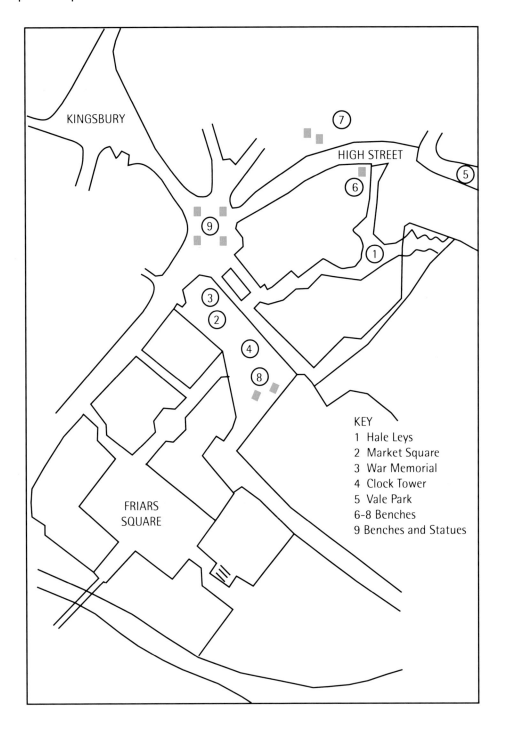

KEY
1 Hale Leys
2 Market Square
3 War Memorial
4 Clock Tower
5 Vale Park
6-8 Benches
9 Benches and Statues

The observation locations

'Traditional' market square: Market Square

The cobbled Market Square, with an 18th-century Crown Court house, a Victorian clock tower, a war memorial and various other monumental statues, lies at the centre of Aylesbury. It is bounded on two sides by the Hale Leys and Friars Square shopping malls. To the northwest, it adjoins Kingsbury and to the northeast, High Street. A market is held four times a week. Observations were conducted at the lower end of the square between the clock tower and the County Court building; in the middle of the square where markets are held; and at the top of the square including the war memorial and benches at the point where the square meets High Street (see Map 2).

Market Square: junction with High Street

Newly developed, town centre square: Kingsbury

> As part of the Aylesbury town centre redevelopment, a government grant has enabled a £1.7m regeneration scheme in Kingsbury – one of the oldest parts of Aylesbury. With an innovative water clock as its centrepiece, the square has a large pedestrian area, trees and improved lighting. It aims to bring café culture to the town and provide a vibrant meeting place, which links the old town with the new. (AVDC, 2004)

Kingsbury is a 'square' bounded by shops and other businesses. It meets Market Square at a narrow passage point, and at the other end it gives access to the old town centred around St. Mary's Church. Before its redevelopment, Kingsbury was 'underutilised and showing signs of deterioration' (ODPM, 2004, p 4) – it contained a disreputable public lavatory and was frequented by street drinkers. During the period of observation it was reopened in its new guise as a piazza-style open space. The square is typical of developments in many town centres in its aim to promote a 'European-style café culture' in the town (see Map 2). The observation points included the lower square below the water feature; the middle of the square including the café seating areas; the top of the square and the bus stops.

Kingsbury

'Traditional' shopping street: High Street

High Street is a part-pedestrianised shopping street, which leads from Market Square to Exchange Street, where there is access to Vale Park via an underpass. In addition to the shops, some formal street trading, usually at regular pitches, is permitted (for example, a fast food stall, an ice cream van, a Big Issue seller). There is also some informal trading from impromptu street stalls, and occasional busking and begging. In addition to the benches at the junction with Market Square, permanent seating is provided about halfway along the street outside shops. Café tables and chairs are provided outside a coffee shop during opening hours. High Street continues to house two of the town's larger retail chain stores, although many other stores have moved into either of the two indoor shopping centres (see Map 2). Observations were carried out at the top of High Street adjoining Market Square; the mid-section area around the 'Smith's' benches; and from this point to the end of the part-pedestrianised section, including the 'McDonald's' benches.

Recently redeveloped/refurbished shopping centre: Friars Square

The Friars Square shopping centre was redeveloped on the site of an earlier shopping centre and reopened in 1993. On three floors, it is based around a large covered square with seating areas, cafés, kiosks and ornamental features, and its small lower level houses independent traders. The main front entrance is on Market Square, and the northerly exit leads via a bridge to a multi-storey car park and the town's railway station. Observations particularly focused on the main central space and the walk from the front to the back entrances, one of which led to the bus station (see Map 3).

Friars Square: interior

Map 3: Friars Square: layout of main floor

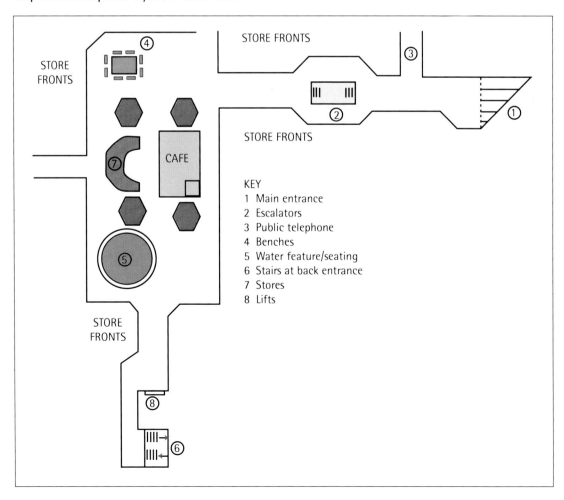

KEY
1 Main entrance
2 Escalators
3 Public telephone
4 Benches
5 Water feature/seating
6 Stairs at back entrance
7 Stores
8 Lifts

Older indoor shopping centre: Hale Leys

The Hale Leys shopping centre was built in the early 1980s. It consists of a 'street' of inward-facing shops, widening at one point to accommodate a small seating area around a coffee stall. The main entrances of Hale Leys are in Market Square, and at the mid-point of High Street. A back entrance gives access to a lane alongside a multi-storey car park. Observations were made at all the entrance points and through the centre.

The municipal park: Vale Park

Vale Park is situated close to the town centre. It is divided from the lower end of High Street by the busy Exchange Street but linked to it via a pedestrian underpass. People arriving by car enter at the other end of the park, by the leisure centre, where there is a car park. At the time of observation, the park retained most of its Victorian/early 20th-century characteristics, although plans had been drawn up for redevelopment with financial support from the Green Spaces Fund and other sources. Vale Park was generally regarded as being tired and less attractive than it could be, and as underperforming in its role as the park for the whole of the town – Aylesbury residents and visitors alike – rather than as a local park for a particular neighbourhood. Proposed incremental developments included enhanced sporting facilities, the restoration of the formal gardens and the creation of specific areas for children and young people. Aylesbury Vale District Council (AVDC) sought the views of local people on what facilities they preferred.

Vale Park: children's playground

The whole park was observed, broken down to micro-locations. These included the formal gardens area at the High Street end; the central sports areas including the skatepark, bowls, tennis and football areas; and the top end of the park around the leisure centre, including the children's play area (see Map 4, page 19).

The canal: the Grand Union Canal basin

The Aylesbury arm of the Grand Union Canal runs alongside Vale Park and terminates at a marina located below the main town centre. Initially, observations were made of the section of the canal towpath that runs between a large supermarket and the perimeter of Vale Park, and a road bridge carrying High Street across the canal. This rather neglected section of the canal ran alongside a large disused factory and included a set of locks. Following the first co-researcher group meeting, observations were extended to include the marina basin. The area remains undeveloped, although plans have been approved to develop the entire canal basin into a waterfront development with apartments, cafés and retail outlets.

Canal basin: looking towards the Aylesbury marina

Public housing estate: Walton Court

Away from the town centre, Walton Court housing estate was built in the late 1960s and early 1970s. At the time, it was one of the largest public housing estates in the town. The estate includes a local shopping area, which was built around a small grassed space, surrounded on four sides by shops/businesses at ground level with housing above, giving an enclosed and overlooked feel to the space. At one side of this central area and visible from it there is a grassed open space with a dilapidated children's playground, and on the opposite side and across a busy road is a large sports field. On the other two sides there is a car parking area, and housing. Walton Court centre serves a well-established estate of largely social housing with a generally lower socioeconomic demographic profile than in Aylesbury as a whole. Although some properties transferred to owner-occupancy under the right-to-buy scheme, many properties remain in public ownership including a number of those in the courtyard of maisonette-style flats around the shops. Observation was carried out around the central shopping area and at the adjoining playgrounds and sports field.

Walton Court

New private housing development: Fairford Leys

Fairford Leys is a developing 'village' community, recently built on the edge of town as part of the expansion of Aylesbury. It has been designed under the premise of 'sustainable communities' and represents the current trend in high-density residential development. It consists of predominantly owner-occupied houses and flats. Its population has a higher socioeconomic profile than that of Walton Court. The focal point of the neighbourhood, Hampden Square, includes a community centre (opened in 2004), an ecumenical church, a children's nursery and businesses, with houses and flats above the businesses to three storeys in height. There is a prominent bandstand to one side. Contrary to original plans, the square was developed to include a car parking area in the middle, and traffic is allowed to circulate through the square. The observation areas at Fairford Leys included this space and a walk through residential streets to a point where the estate was separated from a neighbouring estate of social housing by a wide 'riverine' drainage ditch.

Fairford Leys

Conclusions

Aylesbury was considered a useful place to study due to its 'ordinariness', in many ways typical of other urban areas subject to growth pressures. The public spaces chosen for observation in the town included a range of different types of spaces that were felt to represent those commonly found in most towns, including open green spaces; residential neighbourhood spaces; and town centre areas, including central squares and shopping areas. Within these spaces was a variety of smaller sites, including playgrounds and skateparks, pavements and open squares, benches and picnic areas, exits and corridors, alleyways and main thoroughfares. Similarities between some of the sites facilitated comparisons, which are presented in the next chapter.

Interactions in places

This chapter presents an overview of the year-long observation in the public spaces described in Chapter 3. It is not possible here to explore all the nuanced groups and activities within and between these spaces. Instead, descriptive accounts of the prominent uses and users of the sites are presented, drawing primarily on aggregations of the observation data. Extracts from observation diaries are presented alongside the descriptions to demonstrate how some of the themes discussed elsewhere in the report were empirically identified.[3] In subsequent chapters we discuss the possible implications of, and explanations for, the patterns described here.

Green spaces: town parks and canal towpaths

In a review for the government of urban green spaces, Dunnett et al (2002) suggested that such spaces can be major catalysts for wider community and economic spin-offs: 'The fact that parks in particular offer free, open, non discriminatory access all day, every day and are visible representations of neighbourhood quality were identified as important reasons for their special role' (Dunnett et al, 2002, p 16). This section of the chapter describes how open access green spaces are used by the public in Aylesbury.

Vale Park

It's about to rain, it's very cold. Today we're in the Vale Park. There are seven people in the skatepark all are white males; 3 are young teens, 3 are older teens and one is an adult. Some are skateboarding others are riding BMX bikes and on occasions they talk amongst themselves. The clothes they're wearing are baggy and grunge-like [...]

Five alcoholics are sitting on the bench, there are 3 white males and 2 white females. They share between them nice and cheap bottles of White Lightening, which as I remember tastes horrid. Opposite sit two Asian adults, one male and one female. They're locked in conversation. Aside from these people no one else is using the site. Nobody has left the site or entered in the last five minutes. The alcoholics throw their cans in the bin, separate and go their own way. Now nobody is here.

The weather is dusky, cold, windy and looks like rain. It's possibly for these reasons that not a single person is using the site [...] Maybe in warmer months more people will be using this site. A white female is smoking outside the doors of the [swimming pool]. As we leave she is still here. (Park, 16.00–16.45, 17 November)

---

[3] In the diary extracts throughout the report, words, ellipses, grammar and symbols are produced verbatim from the observers' accounts with the exception of spelling errors. Words and ellipses in solid brackets, for example [words] or [...] represent editing and additions by the research team rather than the original observer.

The thing I notice straightaway is the absence of 'drinkers' in the bench area. I immediately feel more at ease as they are the downside to observing the park. There are 5 young teens chilling on the grassy area – generally having a laugh. The group consists of 2 males and 3 females, one of the lads is standing up and showing off but it's all in good fun. A group of 3 young teenage boys enter the area from the stairs headed towards the park. (1 white, 2 mixed race). They're laughing about something and one of them walks on ahead kicking a football. One of the lads (white) makes as if to go and see the other group of teens but seems to change his mind after a word from the other boys?? Not sure what that was about… This area is usually quite busy despite mainly being used as a cut through. This is not the case today however. The only other people we see are a mum with her two children – a little girl who is skipping next to her mum whilst she pushes a pram – they are walking out of the park. The little girl is chattering about what they're having for tea! Bless.

There are loads of teens at the skatepark I estimate (difficult to count as they keep moving!) about 23 kids which is quite a lot considering its early evening time. I've got used to observing the park finally – I feel a lot less conspicuous anyway. There is a rowdy group of young teens gathered in the bandstand (4 guys, 3 girls). 2 of the lads are back and are making the most noise! They're all smoking, including the girls, and drinking cans of coke. One of the boys (white) moves further away to kick a football but seems to be aiming it at his 'friends' heads. The area is quite busy. […] The playground isn't very busy – there are just 3 kids playing and they're old enough to not be supervised. […] Two young teens sit near us on the steps. By the look of their wet hair they've been swimming together – perhaps on a date? Bless! (Park, 18.00–18.45, 16 August)

Map 4: Vale Park

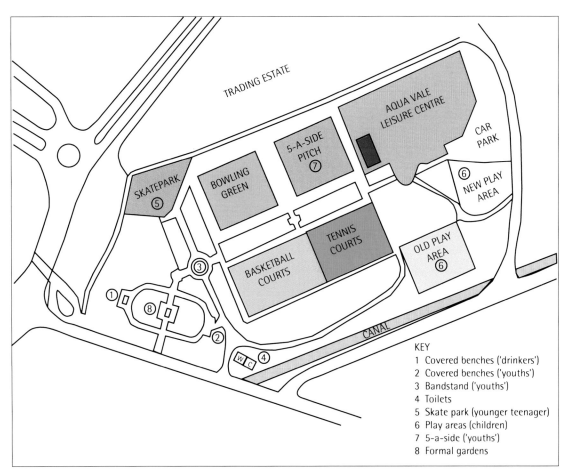

KEY
1 Covered benches ('drinkers')
2 Covered benches ('youths')
3 Bandstand ('youths')
4 Toilets
5 Skate park (younger teenager)
6 Play areas (children)
7 5-a-side ('youths')
8 Formal gardens

Vale Park: students relaxing over lunch

Seasonality, time of day and the prevailing weather and light conditions affected how people used the park more than in any other place in the study. As well as a destination in itself, it was also used to some extent as a shortcut by people passing en route to and from the town centre and nearby secondary schools and the adjacent retail park. In winter the park was occupied very little during the day other than by groups of 'street drinkers'; customers going to and from the leisure centre; and occasional secondary school students. During summer the park was used whatever the weather by many people. After dark and at weekends it was often deserted, often even devoid of people passing through.

In line with the town's demographic profile, most park users were white, but there was a sizeable minority of Asian male youths and young men using the park. Women walked through the park during the daytime, often alone, and in the summer lone women might sit in various parts of the park. They were more likely than men to accompany small children in the park, especially in good weather. But in general, males dominated the park, particularly when they gathered in groups.

Older people were almost entirely absent from the park during the winter and in the evenings and used the park infrequently in the summer. When observed, older people were usually with young children in the area around the leisure centre and children's play area. They did not often use the seating in the formal garden where the drinkers gathered, nor the tennis courts, nor the bowling green. In fact the bowling green was hardly ever used by anybody.

During summer days the park filled up with teenagers and children/families. Primary and secondary school-aged students used the park almost daily during the summer, including after school, and from around 1pm during holiday periods, often staying until nightfall. People of this age were also often seen in the park during term-time in school hours – some 'legitimately' on lunch breaks, others not.

Vale Park: covered benches

To some extent, the 'official' layout of the park determined the key activities that could take place and the age groups that engaged with specific spaces (see Map 4). However, observation across the year showed that people used the physical attributes of the park for uses that did not always fit with the park regulations. These included, in spite of prohibitory notices, playing football on the tennis courts, cycling on the paths and drinking alcohol on the grass or the benches in the formal garden areas. Some people tended to 'adopt' parts of the park as personal meeting places – such as teenagers sitting in the bandstand, and more generally, particular groups 'misusing' places seemingly designed (or interpreted by observers as being designed) for others:

> Rain. Freezing. Despite the weather, there are some teenagers playing on the children's area. The teenagers are in one group, 4 girls. (Park, 14.00–15.00, 20 November)

Aside from people just passing through, the most consistent users of the park were the group of street drinkers and homeless and unemployed people who primarily used the benches in the formal garden area, and groups of young people from secondary school age to young adulthood. Apart from the park-keeper's presence, the park was relatively free from surveillance, and these two groups of regulars in particular made use of the privacy afforded by this public place. During daylight, the park was one of the two areas in the town (the other being a local centre) where (heterosexual) intimacy was observed, almost exclusively among young people.

The canal towpath

Depending on the weather and time of year, people used the canal towpath in different ways. In winter the towpath by the locks was rarely used except by people walking dogs, and observers wondered whether there was any point in continuing to observe it. However, observations at the canal continued and over the summer they extended over a

Canal: towpath and bridge

much longer stretch of path. During the summer months the canal and the towpath were used by many more people for a variety of purposes (discussed more fully in Chapter 6).

The canal was one of the few places where strangers often interacted with each other as well as with their surroundings. For example, many observers commented that uniquely there, people often said hello to them, or at least acknowledged them with a nod; yet they were never asked what they were doing there – perhaps indicative that the canal is a site for 'alternative' or 'private' activities. Several observers commented on how people passed each other on the narrow towpath, and specifically whether or not eye contact was made. They suggested that some people passed by using 'town etiquette' – avoiding eye contact, moving aside to make space on the narrow path, and pointedly not interfering. Others appeared to use 'country etiquette' – a smile, a nod or a 'hello':

> It's a terrible shame that people don't interact. The exception was on the canal, where people do smile and say hello. I think maybe it was because it was quite a confined space, or a more countryside feel to it. Most people if you smiled at them there, they responded. I smile at people in any case, and people were happier to reciprocate along the canal, but I don't know why. I had never walked along the canal before and was nervous about it, because I thought I'd be a bit vulnerable down there, but in fact it was fine. (Observer's comment during debrief)

The observations and the observers' comments on them, together with the survey and interview data on these green spaces in Aylesbury, indicate the pivotal role that they play in the life of the town and particularly in the non-commercial leisure use of public space. These are places where people can spend time without spending money. In contrast to highly regulated commercial town centres, they tend to be lightly managed and permissive of minor misdemeanours and social experimentation. In addition to providing the green 'lungs' of urban areas, green spaces can also be places where people can occasionally behave in less formal ways. This means that such places can also have an edge of insecurity for some, and this issue is discussed more fully in Chapter 6.

Commercial and civic places: high streets and town squares

Town centre: heading for a night on the town

Announcing the publication in March 2005 of a new planning policy statement for town centres, the Planning Minister declared: 'The creation of thriving town centres that provide local people with retail, leisure and other facilities they need is of critical importance to our vision of sustainable communities.... Well-planned towns will attract visitors and investors and can help combat social exclusion' (ODPM, 2005b). The rhythms of Aylesbury town centre and its constituent parts are considered below.

Aylesbury town centre

The following quotations describe the use of Aylesbury town centre by different groups in the community, reflecting the rhythm of the day and evening:

> There are lots of people sitting on the tables outside [the cafés]. The tables have sun shades on some of them. There are all ages and races – family groups, couples and friends. There are several children playing in the fountains. There are 2 boys on skateboards and 3 boys on rollerblades. They are quite young and practising tricks. Children are kicking and splashing in the fountains. One little boy is only wearing pants and a head scarf and is stood right over one of the little fountains and is getting very wet. The boys on roller blades have now found a big piece of polystyrene from a skip and they are hitting each other over the head with it. It splits up and then they play fight with all the bits. One says 'we ought to put it back in the skip as it is making a mess'. There are some more little boys in swimming trunks playing in the water fountain. A group of 5 children and an adult sit in the shade eating. One man came and asked us what we were doing. He told us he was cycling and a lorry came past and his hat got knocked off his head – his head was now very sunburnt. He said he had just been into the [shop] to get an update on the weather and it was 31°C today. He was drinking a can of beer to

cheer himself up but admitted it wasn't a good idea as it would dehydrate him! (Kingsbury, 14.05–14.20, 17 July)

Tonight is very lively in Market Square. Many groups walk up and down the square – lads getting cash from Barclays, taxis stopping, a constant flow of cars. A group of teenagers/young adults has just come out of a big taxi. They're walking towards the pubs near the cinema. A single man (Asian) is walking by himself with a Tesco bag in hand. Everybody else is dressed up. The girls have high heels. It still feels like summer although there's a bite to the air. I noticed (as we parked our car) that lots of people are arriving now as the clubs open. I told [fellow observer] that we should go clubbing instead of working … shame we're not dressed up! A group of young adults (3 boys/1 girl) are deciding on what to do 'Are you going home?' Then, they decide to go together (to the club I think). The girls are looking very glamorous. I feel like a real tramp. In fact, we're sitting down, all I need to do is extend my hand and I'm certain someone will give me a few pennies! Two bikes have gone up the road … very noisy – Everybody seems to have so much energy and so little care. They are just young and happy and chatting and there doesn't seem to be any violence like we see on TV. But maybe it's too early. The music coming from a car is pretty loud. The driver is driving slowly.

The music from the night club is great! 'Saturday Night …   … Be my baby'… I feel like dancing now. Everything is slightly quiet now. I think a lot of people decide to meet at 9pm, then, they disperse themselves into pubs and nightclubs. A girl is telling her boy?friend 'fucking hell, I can't walk on these things' (cobbles) … She's wearing high heels. The two bikes have driven really fast down the road. A couple of guys had to jump over the chain for safety. I can hear giggles. Two boys (Mexican looking) are looking at a thin girl who's walking with an older man. She turns to look at them and they look at her too. (Market Square, 21.00–21.30, 23 September)

Of all the sites, the two town squares and the High Street appeared to be the ones where all sections of the 'community' – young and old, people of different ethnicities, cultures and social groups – were often around at the same time, and of these Market Square appeared the most 'inclusive' of all. These were also sites where the rhythms of the 'economically determined' day could be observed. Yet when there was no market, most of the square remained empty. The lower square by the Crown Court in particular was very little used and few people ever lingered or sat on the benches there. When markets were held, they dominated the central area of the square. Early in the morning as stallholders set up, they chatted to each other, fetched coffee and looked after one another's stalls. The early customers were predominantly older people, until around 10am when mothers with preschool-aged children began to appear. By 11am the market was in full swing and at its busiest. By lunchtime office workers appeared, most passing through the square on their way to lunch, but in pleasant weather also sitting on one of the benches around the square. By mid-afternoon, most of the older customers had gone. School children began to arrive after 3.30pm, not so much to shop as to pass through to the bus station, lingering with friends. The market traders began to pack up from 4pm onwards and by 5.30pm, all but the flower stall had gone. Occasionally younger people were seen playing football and cycling around the empty square in the evenings in spring and summer. Similarly, the High Street was also frequently deserted by 6pm except for occasional groups of young people.

By observing over the course of a day, it also became possible to watch the change in direction of people walking through. In the mornings almost all pedestrian traffic passed down the square from Kingsbury towards the court building. In the middle of the day, the flow became more chaotic, but with the dominant flow of people being between the two shopping centres. By 5pm, the flow between the centres almost stopped, while movement from the bottom to the top of the square (opposite to the morning flow) began again. At

Market Square at night

night, the flow was almost always between the top and bottom of the square, as customers walked between the pubs and clubs.

In the redevelopment of Kingsbury, in additional to the physical improvements, public order measures were introduced including the designation, by order, of Aylesbury town centre as an area where alcohol may not be consumed publicly (1998 Crime and Disorder Act). To facilitate communication, the town centre management officials established a local business group to liaise with residents, contractors and public sector agencies and the redevelopment was followed closely by the old town residents' association. Once open, for most of the winter the square was little used during the day except by people passing through, going to particular businesses around the square or coming specifically to look at the redevelopment. A few people lingered at the benches or perched on the edge of the new water feature, but most moved between the warmth of buildings as quickly as possible. By late spring the square had begun to attract more people, particularly during the lunch period, when people would arrive to sit either with sandwiches on one of the benches, or to eat at outdoor café tables. However, in the mornings, it remained empty:

> More pigeons paddling [in the water] than people. A few deliveries. Two ladies sitting outside [café] looking very chilly with coffee and breakfast. Generally very quiet and definitely no buzz. (Kingsbury, 9.00–10.00, 22 July)

As outdoor public spaces in public ownership, these kinds of places are at the heart of the public life of towns. The study shows that although most residents and visitors use these places some of the time, and that they are sites where people can encounter both difference and familiarity, there are also, at other times, specific disincentives for some groups. These are considered in more detail in Chapter 5.

Town centre shopping malls

Friars Square: weekend

Weather – sunny and windy ... (we have had torrential downpours and also showers throughout the day).... Down come the shutters at BHS. They beep. But a man with a briefcase goes in, and more laden shoppers come out of the half open door. [The department store] shutters are going down and two security guards stand outside chatting. The one in the white shirt is a [shopping centre] security guard, the one in the grey shirt is from [the department store]. The fountain is a mere trickle but when we walked by an Asian lady was splashing the water gently onto the hand of a small boy. He was obviously enjoying it. A few people sit around the fountain. People are coming from work. Some have work ID cards with photos hanging round their necks. The men often are wearing suits and carrying briefcases. A group of young people are near us. One holds a fag but doesn't light up. The BHS half open shutter slowly closes and thuds gently on the ground. There is quite a bit of litter round the fountain area, plastic, a [drink] can, torn up paper, sweet wrappers. Nearly all the shops have closed. Shutters have been gradually coming down, most silently. You look and the shop is open, you look again and the shutters are down. The shopping centre is definitely closing up for the night.

   People are constantly coming through the back doors, on their way out from work or the council offices etc. They are all ages and mostly quite smart in work clothes and holding briefcases, smart handbags. I can hear an emergency services vehicle in the street. The staff from [the department store] leave by a back entrance. As there is a large number of people coming from shops I presume most shops have a back entrance. Two messages come over the system. The first is to tell us that [the shopping centre] is open for shopping on Sundays – the second to tell us that the centre will be closing in 15 minutes – quite a contrast of messages in a way. There is two-way traffic. Smart people coming in this way en-route to the carpark, and more casually dressed ones with shopping leaving by the entrance/exit. The security guards walk to the lift talking among themselves about locking up. The lift takes them out of sight. The wretched musak keeps on. (Friars Square, 17.00–18.00, 7 July)

As indoor venues the malls were largely protected from the weather and people used them all the year round – occasionally going inside just to get out of the rain or cold – and often tending to linger compared to people passing quickly through the open streets in bad weather. People passed through the shopping centres on their way to and from work, school and other business in the town centre at predictable times of working day (before 9am, between 12am and 2pm and after 4pm). Leisure use (for casual shopping, browsing and meeting friends) took over at other times, particularly on Sundays), when family groups appeared to be taking a leisurely stroll around the centres as they 'shopped'. Older Asian women who were not otherwise much in evidence were included in these groups. The shopping centres were also the most highly regulated places in the town, with security guards in the shopping malls, and bouncers outside particular venues at night; this aspect is discussed in Chapter 7.

Residential areas and neighbourhood centres

The public life of towns is not conducted in town centres alone, but also in 'local' public areas and streets. Small parades of out-of-town shops and amenities often provide a physical focal point for neighbourhoods, sometimes including a local meeting place, whether a pub, café, community centre, leisure centre or post office. The relationships between adjacent neighbourhoods are sometimes played out in these places, often involving groups of young people in conflicts or demonstrations of 'ownership' and territoriality. The two neighbourhood centres in this study contrast in physical design and in the social and economic demographics of the local populations they serve. However, in addition to housing, they both offer shops, catering and social amenities, with central spaces based around 'squares'. The two neighbourhoods are just a few miles apart, and both are a short car or bus journey from Aylesbury town centre.

Walton Court: central area

Walton Court

It's a Friday evening, it has been a lovely hot day but now there is lightning overhead and the rain is coming down. The field and children's play area are deserted and we are concentrating on the shopping centre. There is now thunder overhead. There are 8 groups of mixed young youths and a lively atmosphere. A large, mainly male group of approx 8 is congregated outside the video store and we can hear laughing and shouting. A smaller group of 6 (2 teenage girls and 4 teenage boys) are chatting by the Indian takeaway. Another youth passes them by and asks if they are going to Town. He uses the F word a couple of times to express himself. The rain is now coming down harder. (Walton Court, 21.00–22.00, 9 September)

Well, here I am again and today has a much better feel to the place. The water that came down the other night during the storm has vanished and the birds are singing noisily. There's even a feel of a holiday village here this morning. Two young girls are outside the café chatting. An older couple are walking their granddaughter, a man and woman are chatting outside the fish and chip shop. A man has just gone into the chemist, might be waiting for his prescriptions. People are walking around, one has bought a pint of milk. (Walton Court, 11.00–12.00, 1 July)

We didn't stop, there was a large group of youths around a table and benches. We didn't want to make them feel 'watched' or uncomfortable. As we walked past we made mental notes. They seemed huddled, happy and harmless, around them were a few bikes scattered where they fell. The atmosphere was of friendliness and comfort, of youthful optimism, a group that were comfortable with each other with a gentle hub-bub of voices.

As we are making our notes there are jovial shouts of 'fuck' but with no angst. Perhaps if I were alone my attitude towards them would be more of apprehension. [...] A young teen rides past with a toddler sitting on the frame of his bike. I wonder what his mum is doing. This is a very young area, I would say no one is over the age of 20 – I feel positively old! [...] As we left the area 3 muscley tight topped males, very dark – maybe mixed race, were chatting up a petite blonde haired white girl, it made her look very vulnerable but confident. (Walton Court, 20.30–21.30, 2 September)

The shopping area and the playing fields at Walton Court were used routinely by people of all ages going about their business, to and from their homes, and walking the dogs. During the daytime, lone adult shoppers and shop assistants often used the grassed area to sit and eat sandwiches or have a cigarette and a chat with friends. The shops and the Healthy Living Centre attracted people every day and unless the weather was bad, so did the fish and chips shop and the off-licence in the early evenings.

Signs forbidding games and skateboarding were routinely ignored by young people, but for most of the time this did not seem to bother other users. Occasionally, hectic and rowdy games forced other people to alter their routes to keep out of the way. Young people suggested that they came to this central space because there was 'nowhere else to go'. The groups tended to comprise boys and girls or young men and women of roughly similar ages. At times (usually in the evenings) these groups could become very large with up to 20 or more people. In these cases, this was interpreted as threatening and put off some adults from coming into the shopping area.

Walton Court: friends gather on the green

> The atmosphere is very dominated by this young group, who are joined by more teenagers who fade in and out of conversation and sight of the shopping centre. Very raised voices, and over taken area – feels less safe to sit here, than in other observation areas I have completed, mainly due to lack of escape routes and enclosed environment. (Walton Court, 19.30, 18 January)

As in Vale Park, young people could apparently safely engage here in disallowed activities such as underage drinking, smoking and meeting people of the opposite sex. However, for local children and young people this space was close to home. Presumably for some there was a danger of any bad behaviour being reported. Some of the older young people thought that any trouble usually involved people from other places who came into the area 'looking for trouble', shoplifting and creating graffiti, which they couldn't easily do closer to their own homes. These local young people said that they felt safe in this area but not in the adjacent neighbourhoods, where different 'gangs' of young people controlled public spaces located there.

During the study period, vandalised equipment on the playground was demolished, according to local people, because it had been badly abused by older children. New equipment was substituted after the period of observation. Despite its dilapidated state during the observations, the playground had been seen as a safe place for local children to play and when primary school-aged children used it they were left unsupervised, suggesting that parents had some confidence in its safety. Children and young people up to early secondary school age often left their bicycles and tricycles unattended when they went into the shops. In spite of the reputation for petty crime and disorder, for most of the daytime, both older and younger local people appeared confident about using these spaces.

Fairford Leys

We walk past the village shop which always seems to be busy. In the square/ village centre we pass a woman about 30ish in age. She doesn't seem to want to make eye contact despite me smiling at her. There is some litter on the floor (this is quite usual around the shop area). As we walk along we see a large group of children riding on their bikes. They all seem to be together, following one another talking and laughing, both boys and girls. Two of the lads that are further behind are scared of a dog which is with its owner getting into a car. The man grabs the barking dog by the collar and makes it get into the waiting car, the boys ride off very quickly saying how frightened they were. It's quite windy tonight. I can hear children playing but not sure where they are, possibly hidden by bushes some distance away.

It's getting quite dusk now and is very quiet the further we get from the village centre. We see a number of parents walking with young boys (it would seem there is a local boy cub group), we see a man and a little lad, a mum and her son also one mum with a boy, a little girl riding her bike with a toddler in a buggy, all walking towards the underpass (which I really hate), it's so dark and has a low roof and the lights aren't on yet. You can see where it's been raining and the water had collected beneath the temporary walkway.

Further on we can hear traffic from the nearby main road. We've separated from the families going with the children to their cub meeting. After this we don't see anyone. The area is very quiet, but there is evidence of people in their houses in kitchens. We see quite a few people driving cars too, I assume they are going home from work. We see a young teenager walking and smiling to himself. He seems to have ear phones in listening to music. We say hello to a man getting out of his car with shopping. He has a small lad of about 3 years old. We chat. I ask him how long he's lived at Fairford Leys – he says three years/I ask him if he likes it and he says 'yes'. I have found it more friendly this time (the mum with the baby in the buggy said 'hello' earlier). [...] We don't see many people at all walking back. Just a woman going into her house and a man reversing back into his drive. As we get near the bridge where the play area is over to the left I can hear children playing. We see four joggers, one woman and three men.

As we approach the village centre we can hear a fair bit of noise and see people going in and out of the shop still. As we turn the corner there is a large group of teenagers sitting in the bandstand (about seven or eight). They sound as though they are having a lively debate! I think there are two white teenagers and the others are mixed race and black. There's a bit of swearing going on. I'm glad to get in the car and leave. (Fairford Leys, 16.34–17.10, 13 September)

Square deserted. Quite a few cars in the square. Noticed community centre was open and saw children inside. Saw one couple in the Chinese Brasserie, but may have been staff. One adult white male walking his dog (I have seen him during previous observation periods). Nobody in playpark. (Fairford Leys, 16.15–16.45, 20 February)

With the exception of 'officially' organised events that brought people out of doors, such as the 'Fair in the Square' (summer 2005), the public areas of Fairford Leys tended to be almost devoid of human activity for much of the time. A few children were seen playing between the houses and in the riverine areas, but the designated play areas were often deserted. Hampden Square saw passers-by at the beginning and end of the day, going to and from the shops, parked cars and the bus stop. Mothers transported children to and from the nursery, and did some shopping. Although the shops were busy at this time of day, people 'disappeared' after shopping and the square became quiet again. Only during late evenings in fine summer weather did people linger, usually eating al fresco outside the restaurants (which apparently had good reputations). At most other times the square was deserted except for one or two youths hanging around the bandstand.

> It feels like Butlins here! The houses are all the same, the streets are quiet, maybe a ghost town would best describe it. Everything is neat and precise, even the cars sparkle. I haven't seen an ounce of rubbish on the ground yet. The houses stand uniform to each other, each one a copy of the next. Still no signs of life. I feel like I'm on the set of the Stepford Wives, there is evidence of human existence, i.e. cars parked neatly, welcoming lights on in houses but no weeds, rubbish or anything out of place. (Fairford Leys, 19.30–20.00, 2 September)

Non-resident observers regarded the place as a 'ghost town', a 'fake town' and 'resembling a film set rather than a British village'. They commented on how few people from black and minority ethnic communities were around, except perhaps those running the restaurants. In contrast, people who lived at Fairford Leys (both observers and local interviewees), although they might have specific complaints about the development, saw it as an ideal residential location, with the potential to meet most of their needs. It was considered 'typically English', with 'winding lanes', mixing different old styles of housing – including court mews, townhouses and family homes without gardens with front doors opening straight onto the street. For young families, safety, security, good educational provision and relatively affordable housing were the paramount considerations that led them to choose to live there.

Couples with young children often strolled through the main square, but the multi-generation families observed in the town centre were not seen here. There appeared to be little interchange between these family groups, and indeed little interaction in general except for mothers talking together outside the nursery. Older women went to the hairdresser's in the mornings as well as visiting the shops, but otherwise few older people were observed in conversation. This is in contrast to Walton Court and the commercial areas in the town centre, where older people and especially couples would often stop and talk to people they knew. Much of the housing in the neighbourhood is 'family' housing, and the majority of the older people in the street surveys happened to be visitors. Interviews, however, suggested that older people do attend some of the social clubs. As with other age groups, it appeared that their social life was happening in places other than the public outdoor areas of the neighbourhood (see Peace et al, 2006).

At this early stage of its development, the neighbourhood gives a sense of newness – making it 'empty-looking' to some, to others a 'sanitised' environment. However, some of the public areas were neglected or at best 'unkempt' with piles of rubbish accumulating and cars dominating the village square. Despite one observer's comments (above) litter was an issue that united the residents. The main square had not been provided with litter bins, and as a result the shopkeepers ended up acting as 'litter monitors'. After bins were installed, litter remained a major problem, with residents haranguing the public officials about it, but feeling that little was being done. Young people were observed by local residents, who were too frightened to challenge them, emptying dog bins and deliberately spreading the waste. Some local business owners and residents interviewed claimed that the troublemakers were not local residents, but youths 'imported' from problem areas in the town, including Walton Court. They substantiated this by suggesting that the local population of children was much younger than the troublemakers.

> Nobody walking in square during observation time. Community Centre closed. Observed 3 ladies in hairdressers. Fish and chip shop occupied by 4 young couples (at separate tables).
> Play area: 4 older teens and 1 younger teen – all in different types of jeans, jackets and 2 in baseball caps. 1 Older teen sitting on a swing, others standing around talking

and shouting to each other. 1 boy on a bike and another bike on the ground. They appeared rather menacing. (Fairford Leys, 12.30–13.30, 19 February)

It was clear that residents had high expectations of both its physical appearance and the 'community' promise, and the neighbourhood was promoted as positively fostering a sense of community, but this was not evident within our observations in public places. Observers seldom recorded cordial exchanges between people in the streets and public areas except for organised events, with the rhythm of life in the village appearing to lead people apart rather than together.

Conclusions

As this chapter has shown, the public spaces examined had very diverse characteristics and were used in different ways by different segments of the community. The green spaces were not always busy and were sometimes colonised by more marginalised groups including young people and street drinkers. The canal, in contrast to the park, provided 'slack space'.[4] with little regulation, offering tranquillity and nature close to the town centre. The town centre spaces themselves were the most bustling public spaces, with differing populations by night and by day, with daytimes proving more inclusive. The residential spaces on the other hand were quieter, particularly Fairford Leys, and both locations were prone to problems from low-level antisocial behaviour. The next chapter explores in greater detail the implications of these issues and the social interaction and engagement between different users of these spaces.

---

[4] The term 'slack space' here refers to space that 'accommodates informal appropriation' (CABE, 2004a).

5

Social interactions

Developed public space has been described as predominantly adult space (Valentine, 1996), where adult attitudes and mores prevail while the perceptions and priorities of children and young people rarely feature. Overall, the predominant use of the public spaces in Aylesbury was by adults, particularly those of 'working age', with a noticeable absence of older people at specific times and places as described in this chapter. This chapter focuses on the activities of the more marginal groups in the observation sites – younger and older people, as well as those who are socially marginalised – and on interactions within and between these groups, exploring notions of public spaces as inclusive places for different members of the community.

Different age groups in public spaces

Infants and younger children

Except for designated playgrounds, public spaces constructed and furnished at an adult scale for adult purposes tend not to accommodate the needs of small children of preschool and primary school ages. For example, when young children played with the water feature in Kingsbury during fine weather there were mixed reactions:

'I was sitting up there yesterday, and it was a sunny day, a little toddler running through the water getting completely soaked, but who cares?' (Local official)

'No it's just like, you look at it and you think, what is going on with this town? It's kids. It's like it's drawing them, yeah, it's water, there's a fountain, oh, let's go and play in the fountain. It's not for that.' (Local trader)

These comments reflect that the needs of children and young people are not universally accepted as one of the defining parameters in the design of public space.

As might be expected, unaccompanied primary school-aged or younger children were very rarely seen in public places in general. Very young children were never observed unaccompanied in Vale Park, usually being accompanied by carers, in family groups, or groups from local nurseries and playgroups. They primarily used the play area equipment and the grassed area around it. When there were groups of older children and adults, younger children tended to keep out of the way. Young children were very rarely seen in the same part of the park as the 'street drinkers' or at the skatepark. They and their parents only infrequently ventured further than the picnic benches and children's playground, perhaps put off by the other groups in the park whom they might have perceived as threatening. At the same time, the drinkers/homeless/unemployed adults never ventured to the picnic benches or children's playground.

Vale Park: enjoying the new play amenities

In public spaces, small children can learn about social behaviour by observing how strangers look and behave, how their carers interact with strangers, and how to behave themselves in public. Policy initiatives to foster integrated public spaces need to include the needs of families and small children so that they can be included in the public life of the town.

Older children and young people

Older children (lower secondary school ages: aged around 11-15 years) and young people (aged around 16-19 years) were more likely than adults to gather in large groups in public spaces in all the locations and across a wide range of times, but especially out of school hours and during holidays. Respondents from surveys and interviews cited these large gatherings as a problem that could deter others and believed they were a likely source of bad behaviour and petty crime. Examples of specific pressure points included skateboarding activity, the use of bandstands and young people's tendency to gather in large numbers in the shopping centres. As reported here, observations also revealed a detailed micro-geography of the places where young people preferred to 'hang out'.

Skateboarding

Midway through the observations, the Vale Park purpose-built skatepark was decorated with collaborative 'official' graffiti to discourage the unofficial kind (and this was left mainly intact during the observation period). Outside school hours and in the summertime this skatepark was heavily used by groups of young teenagers. These users would wait for turns to use the ramps, or when it got really busy they would use the ramps at the same time, while other groups chatted on or around the adjacent benches, with little evident conflict. Observers were sometimes surprised at what they found there:

'People in skatepark who were reasonably articulate and enthusiastic and not in the least bit intimidated by the researchers. Surprising because they look quite rough and neglected.'

'Young people at skatepark were bright and interested in the project, the world and facilities that were provided, and knew a lot about what was going on, and generally very positive about things, which was surprising.'

Vale Park: at the skatepark

However, from interviews with these young people, and local stakeholders, it appeared that there were problems with other groups of young people especially later in the day, when fewer people were around in the park. A local spokesperson said:

'The park's dark and there was no lighting and there were some youths causing trouble down there so in a way they were displaced from the park into Kingsbury. And it's their way of saying to everyone, look we're in Kingsbury because there's nobody looking after us in the park.'

When Kingsbury was reopened in the winter of 2004, skateboarders were among its most consistent users and small numbers of young people (and the occasional adult) were often observed skating though the town centre, particularly in the late afternoon/early evening and at other quiet times. Skaters would sometimes shoot through town, using particular walls as plinths.

Bandstands

Two bandstands were observed: one in Vale Park, located within view of the skatepark and the formal gardens; the other at Fairford Leys in the main square.

At the Vale Park bandstand, groups of young people, some in school uniform, and occasionally young couples, congregated. Its elevated position gave a good view of the park and provided some shelter from the rain. Here, young people could see who was approaching and though in a very public place, they could nevertheless be relatively private. Girls and younger boys used the bandstand to talk, eat, drink and smoke. This could be understood as a form of territorial behaviour within an informal location where a group develops ownership, feels secure and is enabled to maintain a degree of privacy (Altman, 1975).

Vale Park: bandstand

The bandstand at Fairford Leys, on the other hand, as a tall street feature in a prominent position, was much more exposed. People using it drew the attention of anyone passing by. Young people in twos and threes spent much time sitting around this bandstand, often leaving litter and spilling fast food. During the daytime they were often the only people using the square, other than people passing through it. At night, young people sometimes gathered in much larger numbers around the bandstand, 'being loud', to the annoyance of people living in flats around the square. The bandstand showed signs of vandalism: graffiti, damage from skateboards and bikes and torn-down Christmas lights. Again, local residents attributed this damage to young people who came in from neighbouring housing estates.

In interviews, young people said that they sat round the bandstand because there was nothing to do in Fairford Leys. In this respect it differed from the Vale Park bandstand, which was a 'destination' meeting point. There was a consensus that the bandstand was a costly and perhaps foreseeable mistake. As one local official put it:

'[A]ll the shops that are here, are helping to keep the bandstand going and it's taken a year to build it because of arguments, but since then, kids come along with their skateboards and their BMXs and they've just ruined it and it cost thousands and thousands of pounds. And we try to fix it, tidy up the rubbish and things.... It's like all bandstands in history.'

Shopping centres

At weekends and during the holidays, many groups of young people also gathered in the town centre and the shopping centres. When these groups became quite large, other people walking by or looking for somewhere to sit would leave a considerable distance between themselves and the young people. In Friars Square, groups would sometimes congregate near the water feature where there was space to gather, before being moved on by security guards who patrolled the centre. Smaller groups of young people (and occasionally children) sometimes hung around the inhospitable back entrance of Friars Square where, like adult shoppers and staff, they could smoke undisturbed.

At Walton Court, older children and young people used the central space to meet friends. Throughout the year, but particularly on summer afternoons and evenings, the shopping area space was effectively controlled by groups of youngsters. They played ball games in the shopping area, rather than on the playing fields, occasionally using shopping trolleys as skateboards. Like their elders, they sat on benches, smoked and talked on mobile phones. The fish and chip shop and the off-licence attracted people in the early evenings unless the weather was bad, and drinking (particularly 'underage' drinking) took place in this area in the evenings and into the night. In the evenings, groups of young people could sometimes become very large (20 or more) and then they were seen as a threat, putting some adults off going into the shopping area.

At Walton Court the young people were mainly local residents, meeting outdoors in a publicly owned space. In Friars Square, young people from different parts of town were meeting up in a privately owned and supervised indoor location. Neither space was designed for this kind of use although the presence of shops and other amenities might be expected to attract young people as much as adults. Their social gatherings in these places can be seen as part of the process of forming a youth identity. It appears that practices of sociability – of chatting and hanging out with members of a peer group, impressing others (for example through skateboard skills, or perhaps smoking and drinking) – were carried out in particular spaces at specific times. In this respect, claiming particular spaces and times of the day or night is part of the process by which young people find their own 'place' in the world. Many young people need spaces to be able to gather together and practise their social skills within their peer groups on neutral ground. For these young people the public spaces around neighbourhood centres (that are accessible, dry, sheltered and, perhaps crucially, well lit and perceived to be relatively secure at night) or the park (where, as discussed below, occupants may seldom come under the surveillant gaze of adults or security personnel), provided refuge. Those who frequented these areas commented on how they incorporated an element of seclusion or separation, while also providing a high degree of security from the threat of dangerous others (not least because the young people felt more secure in groups). However, while these young people were often regarded by adults as a nuisance, observations suggested that most of the time these groups were self-managing and generally benign.

Walton Court: by the shops

The park

While many groups of youths were single-gender and ethnically homogeneous, observers commented on many examples of mixed groups and on interactions between groups. In the park, while most users were white, there was a sizeable minority of Asian youths and young men among the regulars. There had been a history of tension between the white/mixed race groups and Asian youths in this area, but during the observation periods they avoided each other for most of the time, apparently absorbed in their own games or conversations. Occasionally, one or two young people would go over to another group and exchange a few words – especially with someone of the opposite sex. At times groups of 10 or more young Asian men (aged around 16-22) congregated in the park. One such group, when interviewed, included visitors from out of town who had come along to be out of sight of their own families and to meet girls. A local authority community officer described local young Asians going out of town for the same reasons:

'You see, Vale Park is local, so they are likely to be seen either by their peer group or by their parents or uncles, aunties, or grandparents etc etc. And they don't want to be seen in bad light.'

Interviewer: 'So they move out of the centre?'

'Out of the town, out of the town completely.'

Rather than prohibiting gatherings of young people in public places, the emphasis should be on informing people about social interactions in public. For example, older people and other adults could be put in the picture about relevant aspects of youth culture, to help to remove unnecessary fear and perhaps to identify real causes for concern; while young people could learn why their presence can upset and worry older people, and think about how to interact in a non-threatening manner, for example through positioning and the use of body language.

Older people

A striking finding was the extent to which the older people involved in this study as interviewees or through observation, either perceived themselves as excluded or appeared actively to exclude themselves from public spaces for large stretches of time. This is not to say that all older people were so excluded; some, including some of the co-researchers, were active users of the town centre. But the findings clearly demonstrate that many older people are unwilling or unable to take full advantage of public spaces. For example, when midweek markets were held in Market Square, older people were around town and in the shopping centres in proportionately large numbers early in the day, often arriving singly or in pairs before 10am. They moved around the town centre almost always alone or in couples or pairs, occasionally stopping to talk to other people, but very rarely gathering into larger groups. However, by about 4pm there were far fewer older people and after the shops closed older people were rarely seen in the town centre. Older people (particularly older women) were more likely to be seen in multi-generation groups at weekends, when families came out shopping. When they were in the town centre and fewer younger people were around, they frequented many coffee outlets. Friars Square also offered places where older people could sit indoors, protected from the elements, in good lighting, and feeling secure in the presence of the security personnel. In finer weather, outdoor benches in Market Square and High Street were also well used by older people, often sitting with bags of shopping, resting en route to the bus station or car parks.

Market Square: benches by the statues

Older people were also seen out and about in Walton Court, but less so at Fairford Leys and seldom in Vale Park. Observations suggested that older people were very sensitive to the presence of others in public places. They tended to be absent from areas that are heavily used by older children and young adults. Survey data reported that they avoided places that were dark or deserted. Older people were reassured by the presence of visible police or security personnel and deterred from using public places where petty crime and disorder occur, and where the provision of adequate seating, lighting, toilet facilities and shelter were deficient. They also said that they avoided venturing out at night in Aylesbury and would certainly not go into the town centre. These findings reflect those in other studies (see Peace et al, 2006).

> Older people are actively discouraged from fully using public places, especially after dark, by inadequate facilities and transport, security concerns and a general lack of interesting activities or venues around public places geared for their preferences. Their involvement with an extended or '24-hour' economy will require positive initiatives by both local authorities and local businesses.

Interactivity

Social status and marginality

While young people and adults of many social groups regularly used the town centre areas, differences could be seen in how people from different social classes used the spaces. For example, older people described by observers as 'better dressed' were more likely to use the cafés in the shopping centres and much less likely to sit at the benches in Market Square. To some extent, younger people congregated in groups that had a class/status element along with a youth cultural identity – for example grammar school students, older skaters, Goths, 'townies'. All these groups used town centre areas including the park, but only the 'poorer' groups (skaters and 'townies') were seen regularly in either Walton Court or Fairford Leys. Some Fairford Leys residents expressed the view that most 'local' teenagers would be occupied at home or in organised activities rather than hanging around the streets.

In contrast, there was the identifiable and visible group of less than a dozen people around town who identified themselves or were recognised by observers as homeless, jobless and/or street drinkers. Having been moved on from Kingsbury by regeneration work there, members of this group congregated by the side of the canal and on the benches in Vale Park's formal garden area (Map 4). The park-keeper kept an eye on this group and when they saw him around they would tidy up the litter in 'their' area.

Canal: a regular visitor

The irony was not lost on this group that while the town centre area of Kingsbury had been 'cleaned up' by the removal of public drinking during the daytime, by night it was dominated by public drunkenness associated with pubs and clubs and the traffic between them. When interviewed, the group of 'drinkers' described themselves as 'custodians of the park', arguing that their presence should serve to reassure other people because it meant that the park was not deserted and they could help the park-keeper to 'look out for trouble' (defined by a range of panic-inducing activities including badly behaving youths and 'the drug dealers and paedophiles that use the toilets') although this view was contested by other park users.

This study could only include a proportion of the publicly accessible sites in Aylesbury. There were other sites with links to the observed sites in terms of who used them and when. For example, other street drinkers and drug takers, and some other young people, were known to frequent an open space in the old town, close to the centre. This area was used during the daytime as a casual spot for play and lunch breaks. The site also had a reputation for large informal parties, especially on Friday nights during the summer, and was reputedly used by predominantly white young people to avoid confrontations with Asian youths using Vale Park.[5]

> The practice of 'moving on' marginalised people such as street drinkers displaces rather than deals with problems. With the support of central government, local policy needs to creatively manage and accommodate rather than ban people from using an area without specific cause.

Social mixing

Both older and younger people frequently interacted with people of similar ages (for example meeting and greeting), but apart from family groups and older people with young children (presumed by observers generally to be grandchildren), there were few occasions

Friars Square: impromptu seating – keeping distance

---

[5] The participatory nature of the research methods placed great emphasis on the safety of the local observers. In addition, because the observations were intended to be unobtrusive, it was deemed inappropriate to expect observers to enter this area of town. Even their presence during daytime may have caused suspicion.

when real interaction was seen between older people and teenagers/young adults. There were some examples of older people being helped up after a stumble or having a door held open, but generally where older and younger people were in the same place at the same time they tended to ignore or avoid each other. They would usually choose not to sit alongside each other if other seating was available.

Similarly, observations recorded many examples of groups that included people from more than one ethnic background, but it was much more common to see groups of all sizes composed of one ethnic group only. In the case of Asian groups, these were predominantly male although some mixed-age groups of Asian women used the shopping centres, especially on Sundays. Small groups of exclusively young Asian women were also seen in the town centre but very rarely in Vale Park. A group of middle-aged and older Asian men regularly met and lingered at the benches at the top of Market Square, and men and boys of all ages met in fluid groups in the town centre areas.

While younger people regularly met together in large and shifting groups, unsurprisingly older people's socialisation largely involved a single person or two companions, perhaps meeting another older person or couple. Older people, even more so than other adults, behaved as though they were particularly inhibited by large groups of young people although in the presence of security personnel or police and in daylight they were generally able to manage a co-existence. In contrast, people of all age groups expressed anxiety about the activities of (predominantly young, male) adults who, it was alleged, had been drinking or taking drugs, and actively avoided going to places where they might meet them, particularly after dark.

> Policy aimed at inclusion in public places needs to acknowledge how patterns of socialisation can differ between different age groups.

Regulation and self-regulation

The shopping centres are the most tightly controlled, planned and formally regulated 'public' spaces in the town centre. Rules and regulations, security and CCTV are in place to ensure that everyone behaves appropriately. Uniformed security personnel were seen in numbers throughout the observations and the mall managers regarded them as essential. The constant presence of security personnel appeared to have an effect on behaviour in the mall and observers saw very few real incidents of disruption. Sometimes children or young people rode through the centres on rollerblades or skateboards, inevitably to be approached and restricted by security personnel. For security staff, 'kids' were the main bugbear, particularly during the long summer holidays from school. When interviewed they felt that the young people treated the shopping centre as somewhere just to hang about, making a nuisance of themselves. Many younger people claimed that the security personnel moved them out of the centres because of their age even when they were doing no harm. Consequently, many younger people found alternative places across the town to 'hang out', most notably the parks (such as Vale Park) and neighbourhood centres (such as Walton Court). However, the gathering of young people, and other marginalised groups, in different public spaces is not just the result of forced dispersal. Certain areas also offered particular attractions for different groups, to meet friends, or to feel safe or undisturbed by security or police.

> We talk about why they come here. They say it's because this is where they can come, this is 'like a place for them'. They know a lot of people who come to the park and they feel safe here. They arrive at around 11 and will leave at 8 ish;

though they will go and eat 'in town', probably at McDonalds or KFC. Although there are lots of different groups in the park – they point out the drunks and the Asian youths from their vantage point on top of the skate ramps – these groups 'never mix'. They comment that this is 'weird'. I ask why it happens. They tell me that because Aylesbury doesn't have many parks, or places to go, everyone has to mix together, whereas in other places there are lots of different parks and it can be dangerous if you do not know which area to go to. (Notes from interview with three young males, skatepark in Vale Park, 17.00, 11 September)

Spatial regulation was observed in different ways across the town, ranging from *self-regulation* where individuals avoided eye contact with strangers in Market Square or where individuals and small groups positioned themselves on specific benches in the town centre to *imposed regulation* where groups were expelled from one site to another (drinkers from Kingsbury to Vale Park and then from Vale Park). Many observers, and some users, commented on the segregation of different groups in Vale Park.

Regulation in Vale Park

Most of the larger groups observed using the park were 'regulars', familiar with other regular users and with the park-keeper. Individuals would gravitate to a particular place in the park, although it was not always the same place each time they came. Unlike the sharing and turn-taking at the skatepark and the children's play area, in the rest of the park these groups would avoid sharing the same space. If it seemed as if there might be competition for the same patch, one group usually gave way to another and moved to a different part of the park:

> Playground: Older teens 4 males 1 female messing around by the swings. ('Grungees' aka skaters). They are smoking and eating. There is a group of 2 boys ('kevs or townies') sitting on a bench getting ready to leave? There is isolation of the groups. Grunge girl moved as a family (2 adults, male and female with girl) come into the play park. She went to play on a [ride]. Family (adults) don't seem impressed. Kevs/townies left the park as family came in. Group of skaters moved and sat on play frame. They were climbing on it as well. [...] At the benches are males (4) sitting and drinking (they are drunk). They are talking fairly loud. Smoking and spitting a lot. They look scruffy – jeans tattered, shirts look dirty etc. (Vale Park, 13.00–13.40, 18 December)

Overall, the park is a socially segregated space where different groups rarely mix. For instance, on warm days in summer it was common to see these different groups in different spaces: drinkers around the benches, upper years students around the grass areas, almost exclusively white younger teens in the skatepark, Asian male teens on the basketball courts, adults and occasionally teenagers using the tennis courts, male teenagers using the football field, children using the play park, always with adult supervision close to hand. While much of this segregation can be defined by activity – such as skating, or children's play – different spaces of the park also provided opportunity for different groups to meet together and in some ways construct their own identities. On the whole, young people in the park appeared to do very little other than 'hang around' or skate. That this was such a common activity suggests that it is a vital aspect of young people's social activity and behaviour in the town.

This segregation may be interpreted as attempts to avoid direct intergroup conflict, particularly in the light of previous known confrontations. The different age/ethnic groups appeared to be ignoring one another for much of the time, with little indication of social interaction. They appeared to be very conscious of one another's presence and actively accommodating each other's habits.

It is no coincidence that the two groups that used the park most often (young people and drinkers/homeless/unemployed people) included some people who were 'excluded' from a number of town centre meeting places including the malls, either by the prices in the coffee shops or because they were underage, barred or discouraged. The regular group of drinkers/homeless/unemployed people therefore used both the park and the canal towpath as places to socialise rather than the more populated parts of the town centre where they believed they would probably be moved on if they gathered as a group. As in Walton Court, young people were also able to use the park to 'hang out', investigating sociability and occasionally looking for solitude beyond the gaze of authority.

Regulation around benches

A second process of segregation that many observers commented on occurred around public benches. There was a certain amount of self-selection among people's use of the seating provided along the High Street and in the squares. Seats around trees and beneath shaded awnings allowed people to avoid sitting side by side and an eclectic mix of people, including some 'regulars', used these benches, apparently to rest for a while or to wait for someone inside the shops. Lower down the street, yet remaining in view, were benches outside a fast food outlet. These were often claimed, as might be expected, by customers of the outlet, including families with young children, but more typically by groups of young people. Observers noted that whereas school children in uniform would often sit on the benches beneath the trees, similar-aged young people out of uniform tended to position themselves around the benches outside the fast food outlet. The division between the two sets of benches appeared even more noticeable on Saturdays, with younger people usually tending to cluster around the benches outside the fast food outlet regardless of whether or not they were eating food from there. A similar process was observed in the shopping centre:

> The [fountain] is being used as a waiting area with lots of people sitting on the rim – but keeping their distance from each other! An average of 6 feet between each person. Is this intentional? A built in measure? A couple sit and eat sandwiches and chat – perhaps they're on their lunch break? People sit and use phones. Seems to be a meeting place too. No one talks unless they're with someone. There are more people on the side [facing into the centre than facing the wall]. [...]
> All the benches are in use – most having just 2 people on – no one comes to sit on the spare places! How interesting – I would! They're mostly being used by elderly people taking a break from shopping – it's Market Day. A couple of benches have young adults on – lunch hour? The site is quite busy – lots of people walking around, wandering – an air of unhurriedness – security guards patrol round in a pair quietly – not obtrusive – just there. Why don't they have more 2-seater benches? (Shopping centre, 12.30–13.30, 10 August)

LIBRARY: UNIVERSITY OF CHESTER

Market Square: circular bench

Self-segregation is one of the means by which people manage social contact in public places to reflect their own preferences on engaging with others and the need for personal space. Provided that public spaces are allowed to be as inclusive as possible, allowing people to be alongside others who they recognise as being similar to or different from them, self-segregation can be perhaps viewed as a process of identity creation, and innate human behaviour, rather than as a challenge to community development.

Conclusions

The 'publicness' of public places is conditional and contingent. Observations have shown that however 'public' a place may be, whether or not it is accessible to you depends to a large extent on who you are – your age, status, and sometimes gender; and the time of day. Time of day matters because of who else may or may not be around; what services will be available to you; whether you can get home by bus. Older people and children are particularly likely to feel marginalised or excluded at particular times of day for these reasons.

Some people may be regarded as being 'out of place' in particular public spaces by the general expectations of others or by the formal or informal management of these spaces. Examples include young people from other neighbourhoods hanging around Fairford Leys and Walton Court; street drinkers in the shopping centres; or unaccompanied young children in any of the town centre spaces. The acceptance of being in the right place can also extend to the smaller areas within a particular public space, evident, for example, in the complex processes of self-segregation in Vale Park described above.

The CABE Space manifesto states that 'Public spaces are the 'glue' that holds society together, the places where we meet different people, share experiences, and learn to trust one another' (CABE, 2004b, p 5). In addition to purposefully using public places (for shopping, leisure and so on) and also to use them as places to encounter other (familiar and unfamiliar) people and events, people also use public spaces to maintain their own presence as a part of the social entity that is the town or the neighbourhood. However, this study demonstrates that the society that is being held together is a stratified one, in which some groups are routinely privileged over others, with those others trying to exert their presence within the public realm. The gatherings of young people in the shopping centre, in spite of prohibition, were a case in point. Whether or not the public presence of diversity is encouraged or discouraged is strongly influenced by the way public spaces are managed and designed.

While the causes and implications of a stratified society are beyond the scope of this study, it suggests that inclusion in public places requires policy makers to take account of power relations in formulating policy on the uses of public space. In terms of social cohesion and inclusion, it is better to please all of the people (including all age groups) some of the time than to privilege some people (for example commercially active adults) all of the time, to the exclusion of others.

6

Managing and regenerating public spaces

This chapter considers how place identity and reputation affect the use of public spaces. It considers some of the key issues for managing public spaces at a local level and examines the impact of the regeneration of public space and the extent to which the social construction of place is and is not supported by the development of spaces. Aylesbury is planning to grow substantially in the near future and the redevelopment of public spaces needs to be informed by public perception of current space and projected needs. Reactions by people using the recently redeveloped square at Kingsbury provide lessons that should inform any future plans for regeneration as the town grows: this could have resonance in other towns across the country seeking to expand while maintaining or enhancing their public realm. Also considered here is public order, so frequently commented on by the co-researchers, and the extent to which it was maintained by the unwritten regulatory 'codes of conduct' performed everyday by individuals when out in public.

Place and reputation

In a district-wide survey of households conducted by AVDC (2001), respondents were asked to describe the community they lived in, given three options: 'a close-knit local community with its own special identity'; 'a community that is increasingly losing its own identity' or 'not a close-knit community with any special sense of identity'. Twenty-eight per cent of Aylesbury town residents responded that there was a 'special identity', 20% that the community was 'losing its identity' and 50% that it had 'no special identity'. These replies indicated a much lower sense of local identity than in other parts of the district surveyed.

The public spaces of a town may both reflect and influence how people feel about the place where they live, and in this study of Aylesbury the persistence and influence of reputation was an important aspect of place identity. In interviews and surveys, people commented on Aylesbury's reputation and image, often based on incidents reported in local (and occasionally national) media and, in particular, past events were used as evidence that Aylesbury is a violent town. Yet although there were tensions at times, the idea that Aylesbury fitted this description or was in any way unusually crime-ridden was not borne out by observation.

Apart from this, interviews, the site survey and group sessions with the 46 co-researchers revealed a diversity of opinion about Aylesbury's image as a town, including views that it was 'run down', 'historic' and 'improving'. Specific public places had reputations of their own. Walton Court, Vale Park and Kingsbury bore reputations for petty criminality, litter and graffiti, youth crime, drink- and drug-related disorder and the presence of disorderly people. Most co-researchers took a more optimistic view of the town after completing observations – reflected, for example, in the comments of two observers encountering Walton Court:

'A disadvantage is that you have preconceptions about a place. My initial reaction to Walton Court was a poor one, a gut reaction, and I had a negative feeling about observing there, but when we got there it was fine.'

'Had prejudged Walton Court a bit (due to its reputation); after spending time there came to like it much more than I had expected. It has a slightly more depressing look to it, but is much more real and interesting than Fairford Leys was, for example.'

In spite of Walton Court's recognised petty crime and disorder, and the reputation that it had acquired both locally and among outsiders, this study suggests that while the presence or expectation of large groups of older teenagers and young adults in the evenings still presented a problem and a deterrent for many people, for most of the daytime local people were confident about using these spaces and they could sustain a sense of community. The design of this enclosed space may make group behaviour appear more threatening at particular times of day.

The reputation of Vale Park is also an issue. It deters many people, especially older people and families, from using it. Additionally, it is inaccessible: poorly signposted and not clearly visible from the High Street, from where it had to be accessed either across the very busy dual carriageway or via a frequently deserted underpass. The park offered little to older people to compensate for the effort of getting to it or to offset its reputation for being unsafe.

During the first few months following the redevelopment of Kingsbury there were ongoing problems with the water feature; however, later observations showed people beginning to use the space as intended – sitting out, café-culture style. Describing the collective action behind the redevelopment of Kingsbury, two individuals involved referred to the image creation involved in that process:

A: 'And this was the vision, this continental thing.'

B: 'Yeah that's what came from all these stakeholder groups, local residents groups, everyone.'

A: 'And you could say well why did they say that, why do they want that? And I suppose it's, I mean Aylesbury in a way is a stage, the whole thing is a show and if you've got a thing happening up there it's just another reason to pull people into the town.'

Poor local reputations led to various initiatives from local authorities and businesses to reduce crime and fear of crime, including initiatives targeted particularly on public spaces. These included physical redesign (Vale Park), security measures (CCTV, community safety officers and policing; Fairford Leys, Walton Court, Kingsbury) and community projects (Healthy Living Centre, new playgrounds; Walton Court). To combat persistent bad reputations, positive publicity is also needed to encourage more upbeat public expectations and responses to particular places.

Kingsbury: alfresco seating

The management and security of public spaces

Issues raised in relation to the management of public spaces show that it is impossible to please 'all of the people all of the time'. The quotations below come from the street survey of Kingsbury and express the wide diversity of needs. While the first acknowledges the need for planning and design to make the town more physically accessible, the second demonstrates the contested nature of space and the difficulties in regenerating these areas to meet everyone's needs.

> 'I can get around a lot easier, I use the wheelchair and it's very flat – accessible … but then I knew all the places to go before to get around.'

> 'Could have put cobbles to stop the skateboarders – can't let kids wander around on Saturdays. Water gets everywhere, very desolate, too open, not an attraction … people wreck everything, people lost businesses – should have done it better … wrecked the trees, where are the flowerbeds?'

Finding ways to keep the central areas public and open to all requires innovation and imagination, cultural stimulation, recognition of diversity of users, as well as access to resources to provide ongoing maintenance of the infrastructure. Cooperation is needed between those charged with managing public areas. Overall control of the public spaces in Aylesbury rests with the District Council (AVDC), but the main town centre is under the remit of Aylesbury Town Centre Partnership (ATCP) – a partnership between AVDC, Aylesbury Town Council, Buckinghamshire County Council, Thames Valley Police and local businesses, including the managers of the two shopping centres. ATCP appoints the town centre manager and aims to 'make Aylesbury town centre a pleasant and safe place for people to live, work and visit' and 'balance the different needs of all stakeholders, including residents, businesses and visitors' (AVDC, 2004).

The two large shopping malls in the town centre (Friars Square and Hale Leys) are under private management and are tightly controlled, planned and regulated 'public' spaces in 'private' ownership. Rules and regulations, security and CCTV are in place to ensure acceptable behaviour. Mall managers regarded the presence of uniformed security personnel as essential and these personnel were observed throughout the study. One manager said: 'I like to think of them as customer service. They're dealing with lost children, the general public, answering questions'. The security role here is seen as part of the overall shopping experience, which is appreciated by many people but less so by others.

Interviewer: 'What does the security job entail?'

Manager: 'Well making sure that our customers' visit is enjoyable. And they're not intimidated or disrupted at all by any elements that may or may not be around at that time.'

Interviewer: 'Any element? What do you mean by that?'

Manager: 'Well it's mainly kids. We're in the worst times of the year now. School holidays, summer holidays. They gather in groups, which we actively discourage, they treat it not as a shopping centre, just as somewhere to hang about, you know. Make a nuisance of themselves … people don't like it. They come here to do their shopping, it's not a leisure centre, you know, they come here to do their shopping and they just, people don't like it.'

The public authorities had also taken steps to manage particular local spaces where safety was perceived as an issue. The very centre of Aylesbury sees the convergence of several route-ways known to the authorities as the 'Kingsbury, Market Square, Exchange Street corridor' and identified as a site of serious concern with regard to crime, disorder and nuisance (AVDC, 2004). On summer nights the presence of many pubs and takeaways there and at the lower end of Market Square meant that observers commonly recorded groups of people spilling out onto the pavement and moving around within and between these places. The area was dominated by young adults (aged around 18 to late thirties),

Hale Leys: security personnel

in couples or in large and frequently noisy (often same-sex) groups. One AVDC officer described the potential for trouble:

> 'I think the starting point for all that is how do we plan out this corridor of trouble? If you've got just one group of people then they feel strong, and with young people, they think, well one thing leads to another, but if you've got other members of the community there, it sort of naturally polices the situation to an extent. They might feel a bit more inhibited about saying, well everybody's getting pissed, I'll smash up this square or whatever, instead they might say well there's people there, maybe I won't. I think that's the starting point for this. Dilute the mono-culture of young people getting, going to high-density drinking establishment and coming out pissed and then getting a cab and a takeaway and that's when the trouble starts. You know, fights over queues for taxis, kebabs and stuff.'

However, observations also showed that organised security is maintained through bouncers attached to specific establishments and police presence at night, with police vehicles or ambulances often parked in Market Square. In addition, community safety officers had been appointed in Aylesbury to patrol particular estates that had crime and disorder problems, including Walton Court. The officer's role was to monitor activity and support the local population; young mothers, middle-aged and older people were indeed reassured by his presence. Some local people believed that this had resulted in reduced graffiti and litter, particularly glass from broken beer bottles.

A physical presence is not the only form of regulation, as activities in Vale Park reveal. It is relevant to note that the management of the park and the town centre came under two different divisions. Vale Park is managed directly by ADVC, and does not come under the aegis of the town centre management partnership or the byelaws associated with the town centre, including the prohibition on street drinking. The management of the town centre area, however, had a knock-on effect on what activities took place in Vale Park as more marginal groups were displaced from central areas.

In summer 2004, a sign was erected in Vale Park outlawing skateboarding and cycling, ordering dogs to be kept on leads and prohibiting ball games from all but designated areas. In addition, users were ordered, 'in the interest of safety, please do not bring glass, alcohol or barbecues into the area'. A contact number was provided to report offenders. All these 'outlawed' activities were frequently observed in the park. Ironically, dog walkers, drinkers and skateboarders were often the only people to use the park for much of the time. The banning of glass and alcohol appeared to be particularly directed at the street drinkers, while the restrictions placed on skateboarding and cycling suggested a direct attempt to control young people in the park. Graffiti was shortly added to the sign. This prohibitory approach, while common, is in contrast to the approach taken by the 'Code of Conduct' for safe parks promoted in national policy.[6] The code suggests welcoming 'well-behaved dogs; considerate skateboarders and cyclists' and 'barbecues ... in the designated areas'. However, the council's decision to put up the notice does reflect the views of a small group surveyed as part of this study during August 2005. When asked what they disliked about the park and ways in which it might be improved, comments centred on the 'drunks' and the 'chavs'[7] who frequented the park and, in terms of improvements, security and the presence of park wardens, the need for more seating and the opportunity to watch sport taking place:

---

[6] www.cleanersafergreener.gov.uk/en/1/pand0safeparks.html

[7] Use of the term 'chav' by some observers, and also some survey respondents, hints at social class laden labelling. But as observing 'social class' is fraught with methodological difficulties, this will not be discussed here.

Vale Park: prohibitory notice

'Cultural, friendly and safe – I have felt inhibited by the winos and also by the kids.'

'Would like it to become comfortable, busy and safe.'

These comments point to a key issue concerning the future of the park regarding who it is for, and related to this, how people's feelings of safety can be enhanced so that the space becomes more inclusive, and whether this inclusivity has to be achieved at the expense of other groups. In redesigning and modernising the park to make it more attractive to a wider general public, many of whom currently find it unattractive or even threatening, can those groups who may be underserved by public spaces elsewhere in the town also be included? There is an essential tension in public spaces between the need to 'live and let live', and the need to manage and regulate. This research suggests that successful management needs to involve a constant negotiation between the extremes of over-regulation and laissez-faire approaches. Public education, information and involvement are key to this process.

It is not possible for surveillance and regulation to control public spaces at all times. This research suggests a need for some gradation of security, drawing on community support and harnessing the general inclination of people to self-regulate to avoid conflict.

Designing and maintaining public facilities

The planning, design and maintenance of public facilities for workable and pleasant public spaces is central to regeneration and making shared places accessible to all. Sometimes minor and seemingly disparate elements of the physical environment, taken together, can define or redefine a place as comfortable and user-friendly or the opposite. In Aylesbury, particular comment was made in relation to the provision (or lack) of toilets, benches, lighting, car parking and signs. The following is a note from a street interview with a local resident in his eighties:

> He is 'very satisfied' by the Market Square. All except the benches. They are uncomfortable, he says, and prevent him from sitting for longer. I think that is because people are not allowed to sit here for long. And then I realise that this is why no one sits for long on these benches, not because, as I had thought, they are in a busy thoroughfare. The busy-ness is another thing he likes. He talks about the benches for a while longer but on the whole, he likes the Market Square. It's not like Kingsbury he says. I seize my chance and ask what is wrong with Aylesbury's answer to European café-culture. It is a waste of money he says, and shakes his head.... He is remembering what it used to be like, he used to prefer it as it was. He pauses again. There are no toilets, he says. ... There is nowhere for an older person or some one with a physical disability to go to the toilet. He is right. And, he says, where would a stranger know where to go?

Toilets

In central Aylesbury shoppers and passers by as well as co-researchers and those surveyed identified the location and design of toilets as a major problem. The toilets at the bus station (at the back entrance to Friar's Square) were often locked and although the toilets in Friar's Square were close to the bus station, these were only accessible by stairs or a lift during shopping hours. Although well maintained, they were at the far side of the centre from Market Square. The toilets at the town end of Vale Park were not always open even during the daytime and had a 'reputation', which meant that many people felt uncomfortable using them.

With the redevelopment of Kingsbury the public toilets were demolished and, particularly for the older people surveyed (as noted earlier), this posed a considerable problem. Several older people commented that the water features precipitated a need to use toilets and they bemoaned the fact that the previous facility, albeit in poor condition and down a flight of stairs, had been removed. The available public facilities were too far away for people with mobility problems and they did not necessarily feel comfortable just using the Kingsbury cafés for their toilet facilities, not least due to the associated need to spend money to access the facilities.

Inadequate toilet provision discriminates against some groups, including older people, those with disabilities, children and carers. It acts as a disincentive to frequenting certain parts of towns. Local authorities should avoid the closure of public toilets and where possible introduce additional ones.

Benches

The usefulness of benches and other seating depended on both their location and design. The canal benches were 'picturesquely dilapidated' and covered with graffiti, yet they were still used by some people walking along the towpath. In contrast, while some of those surveyed found the new wood and metal benches in the redeveloped Kingsbury attractive and good places to sit for lunch, others were disappointed with their quality, complaining that they had no backs. The design of street furniture is important if it is to meet the needs of all age groups.

High Street: benches outside WH Smith/Marks & Spencer

There were some people who regularly appeared at specific places at particular times. They included teenagers and groups of young mothers with buggies gathering at the benches outside McDonald's – but being located at the end of the pedestrianised area, these benches were also often used in the evening by other people who were not McDonald's' customers as they waited for a lift.

Seating areas could also be an important focal points for socialising. The interviewee in the following interview extract notes how a group of middle-aged and older Asian men regularly met at particular benches in Market Square:

Interviewer: 'What about the older generation, do they go to public places in the town?'

Local officer: 'Yes you will see, if you walk in, just go to the centre now, you will find them in a particular space near John Hampden, near Lloyds bank there are some benches, you will see Asian people, not elders, but older, you will find a group of them there.'

Interviewer: 'Why do they go there?'

Local officer: 'I tell you why. I think I'm right in assuming they have no job to go to, they are retired, or because of natural age or early retirement, there is no restriction on their time…. In the town it's more interesting, those people who haven't got a job to go to because of age or retirement, and also they can see life, colourful people around them. And it's what else they want, it is a meeting place for their friends, socialise, like pub type of situation but in the open. Because they will not drink. And drinks will cost money too. And they haven't got a lot of it, so these are some of the reasons.'

The self-segregation of people using benches was referred to in Chapter 5; there were clearly unwritten rules about personal space and people's need to maintain a distance from unfamiliar strangers. In Market Square, some people chose to sit on the steps round the clock tower and the statues rather than sit too close to someone else on the benches nearby.

Because many people need safe seating to enable them to use public spaces, local authorities should consider the provision and positioning of seating, possibly involving sponsors.

Lighting and noise

Interactions within public spaces follow seasonal and diurnal rhythms. Observations showed that most people are clearly uneasy in dark spaces and most spaces quickly became deserted after dark. People are drawn to lights in dark places – many people stopped to look into the window of the one shop in Market Square that remained brightly lit into the night. In Walton Court, while most of the central area was very dark at night and on winter evenings, the lit windows of open businesses provided the places where youngsters gathered. As with making public spaces attractive in other ways, improved lighting is likely to draw in all kinds of people, including those who developers might not want particularly to encourage.

Market Square: the steps of the Clock Tower

As part of the redevelopment of Kingsbury, unusual and attractive lighting was installed and this had been well received even by people who were critical about the redevelopment in general. A similar lighting design could transform the evening scene in Market Square, and improved lighting on routes back to bus stops and car parks might encourage women and older people to stay longer. AVDC has acknowledged the effects of lighting on the use of public places, for example by planning a lighted walkway in Vale Park, saying that 'we expect that, with other measures, this could make a big difference to how people can use the park'.

While in all other observation sites, non-human noise was not identified as a disincentive to use public places, in Fairford Leys high voltage electricity pylons had been incorporated into the development rather than as is usual skirting the housing areas, with many of the pylons standing in the riverine areas, which are used for recreation. This arrangement was largely to avoid the more costly solution of underground cables. There had been some controversy about whether the presence of high voltage cables might be a health hazard, particularly for young children. Some observers suggested that whether they were or not, the vibrations and noise generated by the overhead pylons were bothersome and sometimes inhibited social interactions outdoors.

> Lighting, sound (and odours) contribute to the underlying ambience of places and they need to be considered as part of the physical fabric of public space.

Car parking

The move to reduce traffic flows within Aylesbury by creating car-free zones facilitated commercial activities such as markets in Market Square, Kingsbury and the neighbourhood square in Fairford Leys. However, the cobbled and very uneven nature of Market Square was difficult to negotiate for older people, people pushing children's buggies and wheelchair users. In this case the 'authentic historic Aylesbury' comes into conflict with the 'new, accessible Aylesbury'.

The pedestrianisation of the High Street in the town centre created a car-free zone, which incorporated the two main shopping centres as well as the High Street, facilitating pedestrian activities and outdoor cafés. The semi-pedestrianisation of Kingsbury means that the space is now available for use by a wider range of people. However, some traders have voiced a downside regarding the implications for deliveries to those trading there, while others feel that the pedestrianisation has not gone far enough. One pub manager commented:

> 'They've made it worse because if we have an incident in the pub and we have to eject somebody, we can't just eject them as normal, we've got to watch for cars coming down.... There used to be a road here, and down the other side as well. But, you know, it's the town centre, okay, how many town centres in England now are non-pedestrianised? They are all pedestrianised aren't they? It needs to be pedestrianised, you know, I mean all I want to do is, if we have trouble in here, I end up launching somebody out the door, as I launch them out there's a car coming, I could get hit, they could get hit.'

Walton Court's shopping area is also car-free but access to deliveries from the car park at the rear is relatively straightforward for traders. The Walton Court centre, other than the external parking lot, is car-free and therefore considered a 'safe' place for children and young people. In contrast, and contrary to original plans, the neighbourhood square in Fairford Leys was developed to include a car parking area in the middle, and traffic is allowed to circulate through the square. Observations suggested that parked cars dominated this space during the day and night, even though there may not be much movement at certain times. The following comment from a local official about the use of this square reflects his frustration:

> 'It's used as a car park. And I'm talking with the developers and saying look, that was not part of the original design, the original design was that there was no parking out there whatsoever, but because there's no policing of it people are just

using it as a car park. There are some moves afoot; in the spring of next year we will bollard it off and in terms of vehicle access it will just be used for funerals and weddings and deliveries if necessary. But there's plenty of car parks on the edge. The idea was that this was going to be a space where people can mingle together. The idea of a bandstand was to sell flowers on a Saturday, bit romantic but, you know, and this was a mini-market kind of affair. And that any drinking or eating houses would have tables and chairs out so that the whole square, and the church itself we would serve refreshments out there in the summer. That was the idea but the car is king at the moment and we're waiting for it to be effectively managed.'

Fairford Leys: Hampden Square and the bandstand

The careful placing of car parks can facilitate the use of public space by ensuring access for those who need to be transported by car to an area. However, situating car parks too prominently in public spaces can result in less flexible use and less accessibility for people where cars come to dominate over other uses.

Signage

The public signs observed around Aylesbury included directional, informational and prohibitory signs. Examples of useful public information signs included those on the canal towpath and at the skatepark, the latter with information about young people's services. During the Kingsbury redevelopment there was clearly accessible information about the redesign. Subsequently, those surveyed in this area suggested that having spent a great deal of money on it, there should also be written information about the water clock. Yet in spite of a most informative website with tourist information, there is a dearth of good maps on the streets of Aylesbury that could present its historic town centre as an interesting place for tourists. In spite of its compact layout, it can be hard for a person unfamiliar with the town to find their way around, and particularly to discover Vale Park, the ancient buildings around St Mary's Church or the museums.

Clear and informative signage needs to be given due prominence as part of the accessibility of public places to help users, without creating excess street clutter.

Regeneration and public culture

Encouraging a sense of community by engaging people in activities takes place both in town centres and in local neighbourhoods. Interviews revealed that people enjoyed town centre activities as both sources of engagement and stimulation (such as 'European' market days, children's entertainers and public concerts) and sources of reassurance where attachment to place could be recognised through landmarks, with historic buildings and statues giving a sense of history and continuity.

During the study several events took place in the town, including 'Aylesbury at sea' within Vale Park and a mediaeval fayre and entertainment within Market Square. Usually, publicised events attract more people. However, while people deliberately attended the Vale Park event; activities in Market Square appeared to attract people who were already in the vicinity.

Market Square: an event in the lower square

Regeneration of Kingsbury

The regeneration of Kingsbury is only gradually attracting community involvement. Public dissatisfaction was compounded in spring 2006 when the water feature required costly repairs. The redeveloped Kingsbury is a new public space, not yet fully functional or accepted, and its adoption will be monitored closely by local people, businesses and local authorities as central Aylesbury moves towards redefining itself as a destination of choice. Kingsbury is representative of many such initiatives to create new designed public spaces that will appeal to the broad mass of people. Of the people surveyed in May 2005, 39% came to the square everyday and over two thirds were either very or quite satisfied with the changes that had been made, with many commenting that it felt 'open' or 'tranquil' and that they 'liked the water'.

> 'Vast improvement on what it was – I like the design of the clock and the fountains; nice view of the High Street; nice meeting areas – little bit continental.'

> 'Aylesbury has an ASBO problem, this is a potential trouble spot. I feel this is a worthwhile addition to the townscape.'

> 'Much nicer now, you feel safe walking through – building need doing up, painting. Very old square and painting is needed. Like it now, it's peaceful.'

However, while most people maintained that Kingsbury was improved, several bemoaned the waste of public money, or expressed concern that the water may freeze in winter, that plants and flowers were needed to 'green the space' and that there were no public toilets. Middle-aged and older people were the most likely to be dissatisfied with the changes:

> 'No – I'm old school and liked it as it was. A lot of people will say the same. I clean the square. There are three bins here and I can take the fronts off with a key but other people can't get things into them.'

> 'Some flowers – green, you need maintenance for greenery but flowers would add to the beauty.'

> 'Wasted a lot of money – nothing to look at. Could have done more for the summer months, you can only sit and look at the water. It was always paved. A bus stopped here – it was a lot busier and you could come and use the toilets.'

However, while there was much comment about the changing nature of Kingsbury over the spring and summer period, some new businesses came into the square, and more cafés put out tables, increasing the potential of the area.

Quality public spaces attract a wide cross-section of the public and the consequent mix of people contributes to the vibrancy of towns. Important elements in designing for inclusion include:

- a design that aims to include people of all age groups and social strata;
- a design that draws on public consultation and involvement;
- local spaces that embrace local involvement in their design, purpose and management; and
- spaces with a range of security regimes, including some where a light-touch approach is taken.

Finally, as noted at the beginning of this section, the management of community activities is also encouraged as a part of neighbourhood life. Both Walton Court and Fairford Leys have a neighbourhood 'hub' of sorts: Walton Court has a Healthy Living Centre, and Fairford Leys a community centre and ecumenical church. The Healthy Living Centre at Walton Court offers a friendly café environment with a play corner and outdoor tables and chairs. It allows local people, particularly mothers and small children, a space just to sit and chat as well as look for advice on health and other matters. In the short time of its operation it seems to be well used and apposite. In Fairford Leys the community centre has a programme of activities for different groups, including older people and children. However, it does not have the same 'drop-in' openness noted at Walton Court and it does not spill out onto the square with al fresco table and chairs as the Healthy Living Centre does. If there are no activities going on in the centre, there is no particular reason for residents to linger there. Opening out and extending the remit of the community centre at Fairford Leys might encourage residents to spend more time talking to each other.

Local authorities need to support locally based, relevant activities to help encourage participation in public spaces, which in turn will help to foster a sense of community.

Life on the canal basin and future regeneration

I am not looking forward to the canal tour this evening as it is getting very dark and there is the slight feeling of having nowhere to go except the water! There are a group of 3 lads (older teen) at the start of the tour who are smoking and drinking from pint glasses. They are clearly old enough to be in the pub so I don't know why they would come here to smoke?

We pass the canal boats which I love [...] and there is a couple sat on their boat enjoying last of the summer evening. As we walk further on I wonder where the ducks go to sleep at night as there is no evidence of them here this evening. I follow childish daydream about duck nests and houses!!

I can hear noise from the houses including TV, chatting and some people are even in the garden – not quite the place for private conversations. We meet a couple walking their dogs and we stand aside to let them get by on the narrow path.

There is a lot of litter on the canal tour and tonight is no exception. There are crisp packets and coke cans – all likely to have been left by careless youths.

We then meet a man walking his dog (quite elderly) who stops to let us past and warns us to be safe walking at night. I find this really sweet – he reminds me of my granddad (☺). However it is even darker now and I am quite willing to accept his advice. Walking under the bridges at this time of night makes me feel very vulnerable and I've noticed both my partner and I have quickened our pace. We pass a group of 6 young teens (4 boys, 2 girls) who are most likely plotting where to get some alcohol from! I'm not intimidated they remind me of the people me and my friends would tease for smoking at 14. There is a young couple on the bench further up they have their arms around each other but look sooo miserable! First date disappointment perhaps? We don't encounter anybody for a while but when we do it's a large group of the adult drinkers. It occurs to me not for the first time that they are behaving exactly how the group of 14yr olds were – drinking, chatting too loudly and swearing just because they can. The group is large, I'd estimate between 10-14 but can't be sure as we hurry past not wanting to draw attention to ourselves (note pads lowered).

The only other person we encounter is a cyclist and we move out of the way (half politeness, half fear of the water/bike combination!)

On the walk back the 'drinkers' are still there but the young teens and the young couple have disappeared – on a beer mission perhaps or is it their curfew? We see an elderly-ish couple walking hand in hand enjoying a night-time stroll as it is now officially dark. There aren't many people on the way back but we do see a group of 4 lads playing football in the street (near the bridge). We see the canal dwellers on their boats for the second time and I'm pleased for the first time that the canal tour is over. (Canal, 20.00–20:30, 30 August)

While some community activities need to be managed centrally around points of interest, other activities may benefit from being part of 'natural' space where people can find their own things to do. The Grand Union Canal, which runs through Aylesbury, offers one of these spaces where boats, locks, the marina, the wildlife, houses alongside the towpath and bridges over the canal all provide sources of various activities. In the summer the canal side became a site of leisure (people out for a stroll, walking dogs, jogging or running, just relaxing), exploration, education and play (children climbing trees, a nursery group, children/guardians feeding ducks, picnicking). For many it was a shortcut through town, and people were seen on bicycles or on foot with bags of shopping. People used the path with baby buggies and wheelchairs. They held mobile phone conversations. They wore clothing that ranged from formal business suits and 'Sunday best' to school uniform, working clothes and 'scruffs'. The canal area could be a place of solitude (resting, reading a book or newspaper, fishing, 'just being'), the mundane (people walking to/from home, shops, work), or romance (people holding hands, kissing). The passing of a barge through the lock could be a communal 'event' with people stopping to watch, and people on the path often talked to those on board as a barge passed by. For a small group of people this was a place to live, either on moored canal boats or sleeping rough in a tent on the grass alongside the towpath. It was peaceful and a place to carry out everyday personal tasks (cooking and eating, even cutting hair).

The marginality of the canal towpath made it more open to interpretation than other, more defined places. Observers found it hard to establish what behaviour was appropriate there, and what was not. In addition to rough sleeping, drinking and 'underage' smoking were observed, and some observers thought that they had witnessed 'smuggling', drug dealing and dealing in stolen goods. Graffiti under all the bridges and (as one observer remarked) on almost every static surface suggested that the canal is a site for deviant activities. The detritus of such activities – litter, graffiti, strange 'left' objects (clothing, a pile of books) – and the general dirtiness was offputting at times:

Cold, wet and dreary. Been raining on and off all day. Graffiti on everything that is permanent. Lots of rubbish everywhere and the water is murky as per usual. Not the idyllic location it should be. A lot of dog poo everywhere – even though there are specific bins along the canal. (Canal, 15.30, 19 August)

The time of day, busyness, light and weather conditions had a strong influence on how people felt about being by the canal. Sometimes it was an attractive place; at other times it was an intimidating or 'murky and smelly' one. Yet perhaps more than any other place observed, the interface with nature was particularly strong here and observers themselves were more likely to record details of the environment around them. Observers mentioned sounds, from traffic noises to the splash of ducks and snatches of overheard conversation from adjacent gardens, and were often keen to record the different flora – nettles, thistles, elderberries, blackberries, lavender bushes, buddlia, convulvulus, deadly nightshade, willows – and fauna – fish, birds, ducks, swans, herons, dogs, cats, rats, bats, butterflies and a wasp's nest.

The canal area has been recognised by developers as a 'hidden jewel'. However, a large part of the delight of this site comes from its blossoming in summer into an oasis of natural beauty, from its sense of difference from the commercial heart of the town, and from the life of the marina. In developing the canal area commercially, the intention is to open it up to the general public and to capitalise on it as a town resource, but this study shows that there will also be the loss of an irreplaceable ribbon of hidden 'slack space'. The development-motivated eviction of the Castle Mill Boatyard in Oxford in May 2006 caused great distress at the loss of 'the last of the permanent inhabitants of the canals – corridors of dissent winding through landscapes of conformity' (Monbiot, 2006). It remains to be seen whether Aylesbury manages to preserve the jewel or loses it among the new shops and houses.

Canal: walking the towpath

Conclusions

This chapter has considered some of the issues involved in design and management of public space and how this relates to particular places. It has also commented on the ways in which public spaces might be reproduced, either organisationally or physically through regeneration and redevelopment. As has been discussed elsewhere (for example, Mitchell, 2003), the redevelopment of public space might not necessarily benefit all potential users. In this respect, public spaces might not necessarily be really 'public', but rather serve particular interest groups. It is important to recognise which individuals, or groups of individuals, might be adversely affected by such processes.

There is a consensus between statutory authorities, town and shopping centre managers and the general public that security is a major consideration in public spaces. Most people are observed to adhere to security regulations most of the time, and without this self-regulation public spaces would become insecure and unmanageable. Consequently, and as discussed in the next chapter, rather than present a narrative pertaining to the 'death of public space', this research supports a more optimistic view of the purpose of public space and social cohesion. This does not mean, however, that local authorities cannot or should not intervene in the management of public spaces. For example, the appropriate positioning of street furniture, including seating, and adopting a more relaxed attitude towards the provision of street entertainment, can enhance the experience of public spaces.

7

Discussion

While this research concentrated on one town, the locations and issues that have been studied are likely to bear close similarities to those of other towns across the country and consequently the policy implications go beyond Aylesbury. The study suggests that while social interactions in public spaces can appear to be limited, they involve an underlying orderliness by which people avoid conflict and sometimes feel a sense of community. Many people have become afraid of public spaces after dark or of spaces with which they are unfamiliar. People need to be encouraged to enjoy public spaces so that they can become less intimidated by them and add to the vibrancy and variety that is the lifeblood of towns. This chapter considers some of the observable roles of public spaces in supporting social interactions.

The provision and management of public space

The UK government has expressed a commitment to the provision of public spaces and has acknowledged the benefits they can bring to supporting communities and promoting social cohesion. This research indicates that this commitment must be about more than political rhetoric. Chapter 1 commented on the concerns of some about the creation of privatised public spaces through the implementation of a neo-liberal agenda. This study has found that even in 'ordinary' urban areas like Aylesbury, this is having repercussions on the social life of towns. For instance, it is difficult to deny that the ubiquity of localised legislation, such as street drinking bans, and the management and policing of private shopping centres has driven particular activities into other, more peripheral, parts of the town. The concentration of 'deviant' groups and activities in the spaces like parks has in turn contributed to those areas' reputations for insecurity. It is important to question what it is about these activities and groups that make their mere presence so frequently considered unpalatable.

Friars Square: time out

However, this study hints at an optimistic future for the management of public spaces. It appears that it is not just the physical environment that encourages or discourages people to come out in public, but also the opportunity to see something different.

The provision of difference (through, for example, street entertainment), together with appropriate facilities (through the thoughtful positioning of benches and covered seating areas and access to toilets) may be a much more inexpensive way of creating good public spaces than large-scale redevelopment projects.

Finally, it is essential to recognise that public space will always be contested. Despite creeping privatisation, public space has not been eradicated from Aylesbury (or from other towns and cities). In part, this is because different groups are prepared to construct new places for themselves. Observations and interviews suggest that this construction is seldom achieved through verbal or physical contestation, but rather through a myriad of unwritten and rarely acknowledged, yet repeatedly produced, 'codes of conduct' among groups and individuals. This, more than centrally determined legislation or the actions of professional security personnel, appears to maintain order in public spaces. This is not to imply that such legislation or security initiatives are redundant. Rather, it hints at the need for more nuanced, locally determined politics of public space, developed in consultation with *all* sections of society. Such consultation must not be conducted just in the towns halls or council chambers, but outdoors, in the streets and shopping centres, parks, playgrounds and neighbourhoods. Moreover, it should be conducted at times when individuals are available for consultations; in the evenings and at weekends. Going when, and where, the everyday users of public spaces can be found will locate a myriad of different individuals willing and able to discuss, debate and explain how best to produce a collectively inclusive public domain.

Public spaces as places to maintain a public presence

Public space serves a democratising function. Being in public provides opportunities for all individuals and groups to be seen by others. People who would not otherwise routinely share space may do so in the public spaces in town, and this includes marginal and 'othered' groups. Not only does the process of merely moving on people and activities that are considered 'undesirable' or 'out of place' displace such 'problems' rather than 'solve' them, it actively discourages those involved from integrating with the life of the town.

> I ask what the young people are doing here – they 'just chill, hang out with their mates, play the guitar, sketch and chat'. I ask if they ever go into town – they used to but not any more. They used to go in the shopping centre but keep getting thrown out by the security and the management – they say you cannot loiter in the centre so if you have no money you have to leave – even though they were not doing any harm – they used to hang out in the café or around the benches – not even near any shops but that they were thrown out – I ask why they complied – they say because they kept getting hassled and that it's no fun if you keep getting moved on. If they wear hoodies they are also thrown out and even though they are not near a shop people seem to think they will be causing trouble. (Notes from interview with three young people in bandstand, Vale Park, 17.00, 11 September)

Observers noticed that sometimes the 'drinkers' in Vale Park were not actually 'drinking' – just 'being there'; likewise, teenagers hanging around were doing the same thing. Rather than being in town to spend money, they primarily wanted to meet friends and watch what was going on, but their presence in numbers was seen by many as problematic and this view is often reflected in popular discourse. The same activity can be constructed very differently depending on who is doing it, the time of day/night, or the place and who is observing it. Many observers in this study commented on how odd the park looked to them when the drinkers were not present – because they were used to the drinkers being there, something was 'missing', and their apparent 'deviance' had become a kind of (admittedly personal) 'normality'. It is also clear from the observations that when groups of 'undesirable' individuals or activities are absent from public spaces, then those places are often completely empty. Encouraging people to become 'used to' the presence of difference may be a much more effective approach to the management of public space than legislation and exclusions.

In fact, by far the most common activity noted by observers, across all spaces, was people just 'being there': sitting, waiting, watching and chatting. Fights, abuse and intimidating behaviour were rarely reported. This is not to deny that some groups and behaviours cause discomfort and anxiety among other members of the population, but it is important not to succumb to stereotypical 'blaming'.

Market Square: meeting and greeting

Permitting people, to just 'be', whether in parks or shopping centres, or even cafés, has a number of positive effects:

Manager: 'Sometimes [older people] sit outside our coffee shop [in Market Square], and watch people … or in the window.'

Interviewer: 'And do they buy anything?'

Manager: 'Yes. That's why I like them [laughs]. They don't shout at other customers or throw things out the window [laughing].'

Interviewer: 'What would you do if a group of older people just plonked themselves on those seats [outside], would you go up and speak to them?'

Manager: 'If we had customers waiting to use them we would go, but no I would let them stay there. It's the same with the kids, if they're not doing anything and we're not busy, then it makes the place look full when we're not busy.' (Interview with coffee shop manager)

Towns need places where people, regardless of their age, culture or appearance, will feel secure and free. It is important to decide whether it is better to have places populated with people who are 'doing nothing' than places that are 'doing nothing' because there is no one present.

Friars Square: seeing and being seen

Public spaces as places to promote tolerance and diversity

Observations showed that public places in Aylesbury are surprisingly ordered, but with an order often created through 'natural/routine' segregation. To take the case of the park, while many different groups co-existed in the same physical green space, they were not the same places. Each social group carved out its own particular spot within the park. Just because different social groups co-exist in the same space does not mean that social cohesion has been achieved. Nonetheless, being able to be seen in public – and to be able to see different types of social groups – may go some way to enabling everyone, and children and young people in particular, to observe difference, and thereby perhaps, promote tolerance for social diversity.

Importance of self-regulation in managing spaces

Most of what was observed during the course of the research was predictable, safe and well ordered, yet observers inevitably saw activities that might be construed as illegal or inappropriate. Some sections of the town's population would like to see more forceful attempts to restrict particular groups and activities. While such activities are not to be condoned, the findings from this research should not be taken to suggest that public places should be designed to eliminate any possibility of any such activities through targeting specific groups. The vibrancy of towns, just as much as cities, depends on stimulation and challenge. While regeneration can provide pristine public *spaces*, it is the people that make them *places*. This research suggests that people enjoy going into public spaces and experiencing for themselves the social differences that they offer. While people of all ages want to feel secure and unintimidated, sterile and over-regulated environments are not the most conducive to urban vibrancy and integration.

Vale Park: having fun

Public places as part of everyday life

Public spaces are places for the mundane, the expected and the banal. This important function should not be overlooked, especially in the rush to develop innovative, dynamic-looking places that can often come at a cost to the local memories of particular places (consider, for example, the case of Kingsbury, and the canal basin). Yet this 'everyday' quality can mean that small, cost-effective improvements can be made to enhance public spaces simply by breaking up monotony – for example by providing entertainment and 'attractions'. These need not be expensive tokens of high culture, but can include street musicians, market stalls or something 'different' to look at. Even pigeons should have their place. By way of example, consider the square at Kingsbury in the evening. While the area is strongly dominated by young people (around 18-30 years old), they are not the sole occupants. Observers noted that teenagers, too young to buy drink or enter pubs and clubs, ride bikes together through the square, stopping to watch the display of people. Some homeless individuals who spent most of the day in High Street or Vale Park also came to the square, not to drink, but to watch events. Consequently, the desire to be around other people, and enjoy whatever spectacle is unfolding, is another attraction of the squares in the evening. As with the shop staff preferring to watch skateboarders on Kingsbury rather than nobody at all, the vitality or vibrancy of the urban scene requires some degree of human unpredictability. Indeed, it is often the offer of chaos, chance or coincidence that makes many want to celebrate the potential of public space.

The central story of this research is the importance people attach to the wider community and the creation of 'places to be' – whether alone, as couples, passers-by or as family or friendship groups at all stages of the life course. The interaction of 'time', 'space' and 'season' is central to this picture, leading to patterns of segregation and integration as people seek engagement, activity, communality, tranquility and privacy within the public domain. People have different routines and needs, which make demands on the environment in a variety of ways. For some, security and accessibility are the key factors, while for others risk-taking is essential to ways of living. The evidence of this study suggests that the contestation of spaces, variability and the need for 'slack' spaces, are all inevitable and necessary in the process of place-making. By being involved in what happens in public spaces, people can have a sense of investment that may otherwise be denied to people who feel excluded from them or, for example, because of age, feel disengaged or disadvantaged. This sense of ownership is fundamental to understanding interactions within the public domain and crucial to the maintenance of the democratic urban arena. The necessity of public spaces in the cultural, civic and social life of towns remains unquestionable.

References

Altman, I. (1975) *The Environment and Social Behavior*, Monterey, CA: Brooks/Cole.

Audit Commission (2006) *Neighbourhood Crime and Antisocial Behaviour: Making Places Safer Through Improved Local Working*, Wetherby: Audit Commission.

AVDC (Aylesbury Vale District Council) (2001) *Licensing Policy Statement*, Aylesbury: AVDC, p 14.

AVDC (2004) *Aims, Objectives and Activities of the Town Centre Partnership*, www. aylesburyvaledc.gov.uk

Briggs, A. (1963) *Victorian* Cities, Harmondsworth: Penguin.

CABE (Commission for Architecture and the Built Environment) (2004a) *Manifesto for Better Public Spaces*, London: CABE Space.

CABE (2004b) *Involving Young People in the Design and Care of Urban Spaces*, London: CABE Space and CABE Education.

Coleman, A. (1990) *Utopia on Trial: Vision and Reality in Planned Housing*, London: Hilary Shipman.

Cresswell, T (1996) *In Place/Out of Place: Geography, Ideology and Transgression*, Minneapolis, MN: University of Minnesota Press.

DEFRA (Department for Environment, Food and Rural Affairs) (2003) *Living Places: Powers, Rights and Responsibilities*, London: DEFRA.

DETR (Department for the Environment, Transport and the Regions) (1998) *Planning for Sustainable Development: Towards Better Practice*, London: The Stationery Office.

DETR (1999) *Planning Policy Guidance 12: Development Plans*, London: The Stationery Office.

DETR (2000) *Our Towns and Cities: The Future – Delivering an Urban Renaissance*, Cm. 4911, The Urban White Paper, London: The Stationery Office.

DETR (2001) *Planning Policy Guidance 13: Transport*, London: The Stationery Office.

Dunnett, N., Swanwick, C. and Wolley, H. (2002) *Improving Parks, Play Areas and Green Spaces*, London: ODPM.

Goheen, P. (1998) 'Public space and the geography of the modern city', *Progress in Human Geography*, 22, pp 479-96.

Habermas, J. (1989) *The Structural Transformation of the Public Sphere*, Cambridge: Polity Press.

James, A., Jenks, C. and Prout, A. (1998) *Theorising Childhood*, Cambridge: Polity Press.

Kit Campbell Associates (2001) *Rethinking Open Space: Open Space Provision and Management: A Way Forward*, Edinburgh: Scottish Executive Central Research Unit.

Laws, G. (1997) 'Spatiality and age relations', in A. Jamieson, S. Harper and C. Victor (eds) *Critical Approaches to Ageing and Later Life*, Buckingham: Open University Press, pp 90-101.

Lipton, S. (2002) *The Value of Public Space*, Foreword, York: CABE Space.

Low, S. (2000) *On the Plaza: The Politics of Public Space and Culture*, Austin, TX: University of Texas Press.

McDowell, L. (1999) *Gender, Identity and Place: Understanding Feminist Geographies*, Cambridge: Polity Press.

Madanipour, A. (1999) 'Why are the design and development of public spaces significant for cities?', *Environment and Planning B: Development and Design*, 26, pp 879-91.

Malone, K. (2002) 'Street life: youth, culture and competing uses of public space', *Environment and Urbanization*, 14, pp 157-68.

Matthews, H., Limb, M. and Taylor, M. (2000) 'The street as thirdspace: class, gender and public space', in S. Holloway and G. Valentine (eds) *Children's Geographies: Living, Playing, Learning and Transforming Everyday Worlds*, London: Routledge, pp 63-79.

Mitchell, D. (1995) 'The end of public space? People's park, definitions of the public, and democracy', *Annals of the Association of American Geographers*, 85, pp 108-33.

Mitchell, D. (2003) *The Right to the City: Social Justice and the Fight for Public Space*, New York: Guilford Press.

Monbiot, G. (2006) 'Wiping beauty off our canals', *The Guardian*, 31 May.

Newman, O. (1972) *Defensible Space*, New York: Macmillan.

ODPM (Office of the Deputy Prime Minister) (2002) *Living Places: Cleaner, Safer, Greener*, London: The Stationery Office.

ODPM (2004) *Creating Sustainable Communities in The South East: Introduction*, London: ODPM.

ODPM (2005a) *Excluded Older People: Social Inclusion Unit Interim Report*, London: ODPM.

ODPM (2005b) 'Announcing new policy statement: PPS6 planning for town centres', press release (Keith Hill), 21 March.

Peace, S., Holland, C. and Kellaher, L. (2006) *Environment and Identity in Later Life*, Maidenhead: Open University Press/McGraw-Hill Education.

Sennett, R. (1974) *The Fall of Public Man*, New York: Norton.

Sorkin, M. (ed) (1992) *Variations on a Theme Park: The New American City and the End of Public Space*, Berkeley, CA: University of California Press.

Stead, D. and Hoppenbrouwer, E. C. (2004) 'Promoting an urban renaissance in England and the Netherlands', *Cities*, 21 (2), pp 119-36.

Transport, Local Government and the Regions Committee (2002) *Public Space: The Role of PPG17 in the Urban Renaissance*, Third report of Session 2001-2002, HC 238-1, section 50, London: The Stationery Office.

Urban Task Force (1999) *Towards an Urban Renaissance*, London: Spon Press.

Valentine, G (1996) 'Children should be seen and not heard', *Area*, 17, pp 205-20.

Wilson, E. (1991) *The Sphinx in the City: Urban Life, the Control of Disorder and Women*, Berkeley, CA: University of California Press.

Zukin, S. (1995) *The Culture of Cities*, Oxford: Blackwell.

Appendix
Observations

Observations were carried out by observers usually working in pairs for one hour each session at each site. A small number of sessions were conducted for 30 minutes, and by one person. Approximately 10% of the sessions were conducted by the authors, and these included the very late night sessions. More than 200 hours were observed across the nine sites.

Observers were allocated specific times and sites to accommodate the spread of observations across different times of day, days of the week, and seasonal variations. The actual timing of observations was varied from week to week to allow a wide spread of times within the limitations on observer time. Fairford Leys and Walton Court were observed on average for 10 hours per week. Town centre sites showed the most variation across the week so they were observed between 18 and 25 hours per week.

To give an example of observations at a site, Market Square has market days and non-market days both mid-week and at the weekend, so a typical observation grid would include observations by several pairs of observers and the authors as shown in Table A1.

Table A1: Market Square observations, week 10

		Monday	Tuesday	Wednesday	Thursday	Friday	Saturday	Sunday
			Bric-a-brac	General market		General market	General market	
Early morning	7-8							
	8-9		x		x			
Morning	9-10							
	10-11	x		x			x	x
	11-12						x	
Lunch	12-13		x					
	13-14	x				x		x
Afternoon	14-15						x	
	15-16	x				x		
Late afternoon	16-17			x				x
Evening	17-18							
	18-19		x		x		x	
	19-20.30	x						
Night	20.30-22.00					x	x	
	23-24					x		

72 LIBRARY, UNIVERSITY OF CHESTER